D1245724

Mary Rieke Murphy was born in Missouri, USA. Since coming to live in Dublin, she has worked as a writer and has taught in St. Patrick's College—Maynooth and Drumcondra. She is currently editor of *Outlook* magazine published by the Congregation of the Holy Spirit. She and her husband, Michael, have three daughters.

JUST OUTSIDE

Published by
Lagan Press
138 University Avenue
Belfast BT7 1GZ

ISBN: 1 873687 59 1
Author: Murphy, Mary Rieke
Title: Just Outside
Format: Paperback
2003

Cover Photo: Chris Hill Photography
Cover Design: December
Set in Garamond
Printed by Easyprint, Belfast

JUST OUTSIDE

MARY RIEKE MURPHY

LAGAN PRESS
BELFAST
2003

for Rosemary and Otto,
    you gave me love
    to live

for Michael,
    Gráinne, Muireann and Sorcha,
    you are gifts

'Let her glean among the sheaves themselves,' he said, 'and do not check her. And see you pull a few ears of corn from the bundles and let them fall. Let her glean them, and do not scold her.'

—*The Book of Ruth*

CONTENTS

Waitress   15

A Job   33

Christmas   50

Teaching   71

Baby   94

The Funeral   108

The Visitors   127

The Estate   144

Ø — read

Waitress

THE CHALETS WERE BUILT FAST WITH timber and glass. They ran out of kilter with the natural undulations of the sloping land in their own straight line down the hillside to the purpose-built indoor swimming-pool. Like the flags on the nine-hole golf course, the chalets were pegged onto the landscape. The man who built and owned the holiday complex meant business. A bulldozer had roared in. Its claws ripped up the heather, tore out embankments of tufted grass and crushed the craggy paths that wound down to the strand. Birds and rabbits fled further out to the headland. Local people mumbled against the intrusion but could not resist the jobs. From his own hard childhood the owner could calculate their need. He paid in kind when hiring them.

Mitch and I came across the owner at a party in Cork. It was a casual do but he stood out from the other men. His black pinstripe suit, crested tie and white collar were pressed hard and fit stiffly. Other men wore rough woollen brown or grey jackets, the tweed bulging and baggy. Or they sat in shirtsleeves wound up tourniquet tight above their elbows. When the owner stood to sing he buttoned his jacket, pinched his gold cuff-links and twisted his sleeves, one, two, sharply into place. After singing five verses and leading the voices in a rousing chorus he beamed with satisfaction. His puffed-up cheeks buried his thin-lipped smile.

Mitch was playing the piano, fingering the keys with interlude melodies. The owner leaned down to talk with him but not for long. He was a man who cut quick deals. Mitch was hired. We would spend the rest of the summer at the holiday complex, Mitch playing the piano in the hotel lounge.

A sunny afternoon the next week we drove to the coast to check things out. We were supposed to stay in staff quarters, four little rooms in a prefab building I mistook for a hut the builders' men might have used for breaks and storing things. The doors had no locks. My elbow bumped a wall in the tight corridor. The wall shuddered. The beds were bunks, two sets crammed into each room. "I can rough it, Mitch but there's no privacy. We can't stay here," I said, pressing my arm as hard as I could to keep a bruise from developing. Mitch agreed. After all, we were married only just under a year.

The owner set his chin when we told him. Begrudging it, he gave us the large chalet closer to the beach. We could stay in it until a suitable alternative was found. And though it was not a stipulation, the owner then asked what use I could be at the hotel.

"Back home I was a waitress for two summers," I told him.

His eyebrows went up. He smiled. I thought he might lick his lips.

"But you were a student then. You're qualified and married now," Mitch objected when we left the owner's office.

"So?" I knew what he was driving at—his university colleagues. "I don't care about the snobs. The hotel's a long way away. No-one would ever find us here, even if they were looking. We'd be fools to pass this up. It's like having a second honeymoon."

Mitch raised an eyebrow. But the wanton appeal had occurred to him too.

Five of us waited tables, two girls from England, two boys from towns around the county and myself.

Timmy was short and skinny, given to sporadic bursts of speed with no direction. He smoked his fingers orange and bit the nails to nothing. The thought of his hands serving a plate was appalling. But then he didn't serve very often. He skulked in a passageway off the kitchen, slouched against the wall under the open shelf where outsize tins were stored. Now and again he craned his pimply neck around the corner to keep a lookout for the manager. At the sight of him, Timmy would pinch his cigarette, stash it in the breast pocket of his greying white shirt and skitter to the tables to hover and appear busy.

Jerry never spoke, not to the likes of us anyway. He had ambitions, the most immediate his designs on Ann, one of the English girls. His close-set, beady eyes were always on her. It bothered him that she brushed past and deliberately ignored his intense watching. So he took revenge, encouraging Timmy to scurry alongside her and ask, "Do you turn a trick?"

Jerry's long-term ambition was to make it into hotel management. He had a vision of himself there already.

Every night he exercised it. Just before serving time, after Ann, Trudy (the other English girl) and I had the tables set, he would arrive to stand by the door and play head waiter. He greeted guests with a stiff little bow and showed them to tables. He filled the far ones first. That way he could strut back the length of the dining-room and catch his reflection in the long wall of windows. He found his image irresistible. Catching sight of himself he'd raise his hand out of his tight-fitting jacket and finger his blow-dried hairdo, flicking it to camouflage his outsize ears.

Timmy and Jerry were on the right side of Chef who took unto himself a temperament. Once every night he staged histrionics at the stove, banging the long-handled spoon or fork, pitching his clogs or yelling at one of us because orders were coming in too fast. His trumped up antics were wasted on the diners who, when they heard him roar, merely winced or at most frowned towards the kitchen. But it was not the guests Chef really wanted to impress. He wanted to attract Ann. As the summer progressed and his efforts with her did not, Chef developed a snarl.

A local man, big Mick Crowley, had his eye on Ann too. He sat for a long time every day on a large stone across the car park opposite the front door of the hotel. His broad backside had polished the stone to a smooth shine. Whatever the weather, he always wore the same thick, grey hand-knit jumper bunched above his elbows. A loose string of wool dangled from one cuff. Arms crossed he looked away from the hotel out over the land and watched the sea. Still, he missed nothing that transpired closer to hand.

When not on his stone Mick drove his heavy old black car on messages for the manager to get the post or for supplies. He brought a stack of newspapers from the village every morning after Mass which is when he first set his sights on Ann.

A couple of mornings each week she walked the mile to church. Sometimes she accepted Mick's offer of a lift back to the hotel. She sat tall in the low-slung passenger seat and let the summer breeze blow her long, thick brown hair out the open window. She seemed unaware that Mick's special attention might be wooing. But how was she to know, just twenty years old, outgoing, attractive smile, glistening teeth, creamy complexion? What romantic appeal could a middle-aged farmer hold, he with loose, film-covered dentures, a shock of grey bristle hair and a large nose covered with large pores filled with black oil?

Unless there was truth to local talk which held that Ann was an orphan let down by love and had come to Ireland for solace if not to find a new life. Mick was known by all to be a decent man and was known by a few to be quite a wealthy man as well. He could be for her husband, father and sugar daddy. She could ward off old age for him and take care of him when at last it came.

I ignored the whispering. Ann and I quickly became friends, waitressing the enemy that spurred us together. I was used to a system. You worked assigned tables, start to finish: took the orders, served the meals, wrote up the tab. I knew how to work at full throttle through rush hour lunches and lavish dinners. I could meet the demands of the most demanding customers without a hitch.

This small dining-room, with only one sitting each mealtime, could have been a cinch but operated in disarray. It wasn't silver service, either, as Ann had expected from the glowing terms the woman in the employment agency in the city had used when encouraging her and Trudy to come here. Nothing in the dining-room was coordinated. Chance prevailed and Timmy and Jerry were the biggest chancers.

All of a sudden, for no apparent reason, unless the manager lurked where only he could spy him, Timmy would spring into action. He'd see a plate Chef had put under the infrared lamp, pick it up and with no idea which order it belonged to, carry it with two hands through the dining-room asking at tables until he found a guest to claim it. No matter if it were the wrong guest at the wrong table. No matter if the plate would go cold waiting for the rest of the table's orders. Timmy could not see the full picture.

Clearing tables he was the same. Like a dog on the scent he scavenged among the tables to find an empty plate, breadbasket, sauce boat or stray piece of cutlery to fetch. Though he was thin and small as a whippet, Timmy's arms and hands moved with all the grace of a robot's. He barged between guests, brushed and jarred too closely, then scarpered off on such swift legs, heads were left in a swivel to know what the heck had happened.

Jerry's incursions were also dumb show but they were at least predictable. He planned them. Keeping himself on view as if on a catwalk, he danced attendance on specific guests— the wine swilling man who might give him a leg up, or the pretty daughter he fancied he might get a leg over. His obeisance was obvious, ingratiating. Jerry never impressed.

Somehow Ann and I managed to steer our way through the fiasco and finished up each night in time to join the crowd in the lounge. Local people were not welcome to dine, even if they wanted to and could afford the hotel prices, and they were banned absolutely from using the sports facilities, but management encouraged local men to the lounge. They knew better than to mix with the guests who sat at low tables in comfortable chairs. Locals, their everyday jackets and jumpers curved around their shoulders, slumped over the bar counter or huddled up close to it. Round after round their big hands dug heavily into pockets for wadded up notes and fists of coins.

Once the singsong started, however, everyone got a chance—guests, locals, even staff. Many nights Ann was asked to sing first. 'Plaisir d'Amour' was her song and when she sang it, I looked around the room into its smokiest corners hoping not to see Mick Crowley whose heart would surely swell to her singing, but be left on its own to deflate in the loneliness of wherever he called home.

After six days in the chalet, Mitch and I moved in with Cissy, a local woman and widow who did the washing up in the hotel kitchen. She lived alone in her farmhouse two short fields away. She gave us the second bedroom right across from hers at the top of the steep stairs. Its low slanted ceiling trapped flies on sunny afternoons. They darted furiously when I swung a towel to shoo them out of the knee-high window. It opened down from the top but was so swollen that we could never shove it low enough to get a good breeze. The nights I skipped the singsong, Cissy and I sat in her kitchen in the long twilight drinking tea and eating the brown cake she made without measuring.

When she worked at the hotel, Cissy faced the sink and kept her back turned to the hoopla and she seldom talked to anyone except to pass remarks on the weather. Every now and again she allowed Ann and me to dry dishes for her but our help made her uncomfortable. Every few minutes she'd glance over her shoulder keeping an eye out in case the manager saw us helping and think Cissy wasn't able for the job. Still, she knew all the gossip.

"It's all carry on," she waved her hand in front of her face swatting away stories I brought into view. We were at her house sitting at the table by the stove. She tut-tutted hotel talk but I could see a sharp look come into her eyes if I mentioned Ann, no matter how passing the reference. And she did allow herself one open curiosity.

"What about the other one? What's this her name is?" Cissy picked up the bread knife and sawed slowly through the brown cake even though we'd had our fill.

"No thanks. I couldn't," I declined but poured more tea into both our cups. I took my time returning the pot to the ring on the cooker. "Trudy," I said after I sat down again and said no more.

There was talk about Trudy but nothing specific, just comments. I only trusted what Ann told me though it didn't reveal much. She and Trudy had met working in a blood bank in London, easy mates. Seven months filling out donor forms, carrying away filled bags and hooking fresh ones onto stands had been enough. It was summer, time to travel, a working holiday. Without money they could not go far. Somewhere generations back in Ann's family an aunt was from Tipperary. They tossed a coin—Ireland or the Isle of Man?

In London their friendship had been casual. They knew little about each other. Leaving work each evening they took different tubes to flats in different parts of the city. Once, maybe twice a week they went for tea to a place they found where Trudy could get sausages and chips, Ann fresh salad. Here at the hotel they were the only two women on the staff who lived in. They were meant to consider themselves privileged—they shared a room meant for four.

"I'm learning a lot more about Trudy. Our backgrounds are entirely different. We haven't much in common," Ann said while we spooned leftover jam back into jars after breakfast shift. Once again Trudy had failed to turn up. Ann put lids on the jars, I put them back up on the shelf.

She didn't have to tell me she and Trudy were different. It was obvious. Trudy was short, almost dumpy. Her hair was dried out, dyed dull black. The top stood up in clumps. One side, the other, or the back was always matted flat. She looked out through a fringe of stiff spikes that just covered kohl-rounded eyes. The lids drooped but hardly from a lack of sleep. Trudy never stayed in the lounge after dinner shift, just drank a quick G&T and was off to quarters, I assumed. But for all her early nights her face remained chalky white. It didn't glow like Ann's.

One Friday towards the end of summer when we faced yet another weekend with casual diners on Saturday night and Sunday lunch, as well as the turnover crowd, word buzzed around the hotel. Someone had overheard the manager talking on the telephone.

"Himself is coming, Tuesday next, for the banquet," the whisper spread through the staff quickly. Everyone wanted to be the first to tell. The owner was coming to the weekly fish buffet. Chef put it about that there would be a retinue of friends with him. Speculation about who the friends might be ran the gamut of businessmen and the party in power. Chef goaded the talkers and revelled in their insatiable anticipation, for either he was codding everyone and getting a private kick at their expense or he was picturing the self-importance he could display swaggering across the banquet floor, hat on high, to replenish platters for government ministers.

On the day of the banquet, Cissy was up early. When I heard her close the front door and go out, I got out of bed and went to the window in time to see her going quickly across the fields. She squeezed sideways through a narrow gap in the hedge and disappeared down the hill to the hotel, her short cut. I'd tried to follow it one time but got stumped at the hedge, couldn't find an opening. Cissy was gone early to use the kitchen ovens before Chef started cooking. He wanted her to bake a batch of her brown cakes to serve at the banquet.

After breakfast, Chef came out to the dining-room, pounding his clogs more heavily than usual. Timmy and Jerry stood just behind him. He put them to work, first shoving the tables and chairs to each side of the room. Then Jerry ran the Hoover. Each time Chef thumped his shoulder and pointed to the floor, Jerry switched off the Hoover and waited while Timmy fell to his knees and used a knife to scrape free the blobs of food ground into the carpet.

Ann left the dining-room once we had emptied and washed the table vases and counted out fresh linen. She asked me to come too. From the recreation hall, past the front desk, we carried two long tables through the lounge to the dining-room, manoeuvring corners with difficulty, stopping every few paces to catch our breath or tighten our grip. We placed them end to end along the far wall of the dining-room, covered them with the larger white linen cloths and then went outside for a break. Behind the hotel a road wound up along the hill and then down towards the headland. Wild flowers grew in the grass verges along the runnels. We picked enough for the vases and to make a border around the edge of the buffet table. Back inside we set the dining tables, borrowed brandy glasses from the bar to make candle snifters and lined breadbaskets with linen napkins to hold Cissy's cake.

After noon we washed the dining-room windows, or Jerry's mirror as we called them, that stretched the length of the long wall looking out over the sea. Ann was brisker than usual. She scoffed at the bottle of Windolene Chef left for us and shut it away in the press under the sinks. Foraging Chef's supply shelf she took down a two litre plastic container of vinegar. She sent Trudy, who'd just turned up, to the foyer to gather newspapers left lying about, while she and I ran hot water into three deep pails that belonged to housekeeping. We lugged them outside. Ann poured a hefty measure of vinegar into each.

Steam rose when we wiped the windows. The sea breeze dispersed it and almost instantly dried the glass. Still Ann said we must crumple sheets of newspaper and polish them. The print blackened our hands.

"Mum taught me this. It's the best way to give glass a good shine. My gran learned all sorts after the War when everything was scarce. She said they learned to make do," Ann stopped to explain and brushed away a stray hair blowing across her cheek, using the back of her wrist so as not to smear her face with ink.

This was usually our free time, split shift break, so Trudy refused to help. She spread a newspaper over a patch of ground in the shade, sat on it and smoked. Chef rapped the window. It startled Trudy. She snapped her head around and squinted to get a look through the glaring glass. Chef jerked his hand at her to get up.

"Wot's his bover? We had enough of his carry on last night," Trudy gave Ann a pointed look. Ann turned away and bent to the bucket. She pulled a sopping cloth out of the vinegar water. Without wringing it she slapped it with force against the window she had just buffed.

"Now look wot you done. Still upset? I couldn't blime you if you was. He carried on like a fliming lunatic, ranting at you like being chef gives him some sort of rights."

Ann deliberately said nothing, only swept the window with harder, bigger strokes. Trudy took a smoke from the cigarette she held pertly between the very tips of her fingers. She turned her attention to me.

"Broke the door right down," she informed me.

"Broke a door? Whose?"

"Ours. That's whose."

"What for?"

"Bit o' Ann, that's wot for." Trudy closed one eye, dragged long, finished the smoke.

Ann continued to stretch her long arm in strong high arches, swiping the window with all her might. Mick Crowley came around the corner. His shadow fell on Ann's window. She stopped wiping it. We all said hello. Mick nodded but kept his eyes on Ann. His big hand clenched the stems of a bunch of flowers. The bright florist paper was crushed in his tight fist. He walked past Trudy and me and stood plonk in front of Ann.

"For the night," he said and held the flowers out to her.

Ann looked at him, puzzled. She made no move to take the bouquet.

Mick stood on. An awkwardness stirred between them. "For to fix around the table," Mick said. The air cleared. Ann took the flowers with a smile that Mick took for himself.

Later in the afternoon, two BMWs, one cream, one red, came in tandem and cruised directly down to the owner's chalet. Onto the links, into the sea, then up to the lounge, three couples kept themselves on show. The men were identifiable as being in business, not politics. The wives wore their husbands' success and plenty of it.

"The tips'll be massive," Timmy was out of his corner, menacing the reserved table. He scrambled the cutlery and fussed the stand-up napkins till the folded linen limped and the peaks drooped. Twice we put the run on him.

In proper order the party of six was the first to be seated. Before the masses trammelled Chef's lavish hors d'oeuvres display, the special guests filled their plates. Jerry showed no other guest to a table but stood sentinel just behind the owner's chair. He deputed Timmy to the kitchen when anything was needed. Chef chose an opportune moment when all the diners had been served their main course, to appear at the kitchen door. The owner raised a hand and cocked his chin, beckoning him, then stood up. Jerry dropped to the floor and retrieved the owner's napkin. The owner and Chef prolonged their handshake as if for a photo call. But there were no cameras. Jerry clapped and the diners joined in.

Dinner proceeded apace punctuated by outbursts of loud laughing from the owner's table that kept heads turning towards the glamorous party of six. Dessert finished, they carried their Irish coffees to the lounge for the singsong. Jerry escorted them. If a tip was to be slipped it was not to Timmy so he cried off for the night. Ann, Trudy and I were left to put the room back in order.

Each time I took a tray loaded with leftover serving dishes to the kitchen, Cissy turned to look, keeping an eye to the breadbaskets to see if they came back empty. Most did. We worked fast. Music coming from the lounge was lively. Ann would not have to sing to get things going. When we got there the owner was just walking to the piano. He positioned himself right under a ceiling light. His suntanned face glowed. Perspiration dotted his temples. He let it trickle until after the final chorus when, with a flourish he took the white handkerchief from his breast pocket and dabbed it to his face while loud applause burst upon him.

But it was Trudy who stole the show. Without warning she stood, took mincing steps across the lounge in a beeline to the piano. She sang and spoke five verses of a music hall number. Everyone joined in the chorus with gusto and clapped a long time when Trudy finished. Men at the bar whistled and shouted for an encore but Trudy could not be induced to sing another. Nor did she hang on to bask in the attention. She left immediately, early as usual.

"The big man's happy the night. The fingers were flyin'," Mick Crowley told Mitch at the end of the night when Mitch held the front door for Mick and me. The night air was cool and fresh. We stepped into it quickly, relieved to be out of the hot, packed lounge.

"I do my best," Mitch took Mick's compliment to be on his playing.

"'Tisn't your fingers at all, Bie," Mick corrected him. "'Tis the fingers playin' the till. Them's the ones himself is watching," he cocked his chin and held a wink.

Next day was definitely the morning after. Cissy slept it out. Mick Crowley was not on his perch and I met the night manager coming up from the owner's chalet carrying breakfast trays. The BMWs were gone. Chef wasn't snarling, just grumbling. Even guests seemed subdued. Strangest of all, Ann was absolutely quiet. She said nothing the whole time we served breakfast. And she left early.

"You can manage, can't you, only three tables left? I have to go. There are some things I must do. Do you mind? I'll try to be back to set up for lunch," she said. Her blue eyes did not sparkle. They were intent.

I cleared the dining-room alone. It was a chilly day. The mist was slow to rise but I pushed open all the windows. Last night's air had to be dispelled. Looking out I saw Ann standing where the hawthorn tree gave some seclusion. Mick Crowley was with her. They were talking, seriously it seemed. Later, Mick's car was gone. Nearing noon I set the tables, filled jugs with water and lemon slices, fixed bread rolls in baskets and set out the coffee and tea paraphernalia. Ann was not back. There was no sign of Trudy who would normally have been here by now to start her day with black coffee.

"They've packed her off," I heard Timmy's voice. He was coming up the stairs towards the dining-room. Jerry was with him.

"About time," he huffed.

"Caught her ... " Timmy saw me. He stopped. So did the talking. He grinned at me in a taunting way, like he had a secret he wasn't going to tell. I stared him in the eye. He shifted his look past me, over my shoulder and must have seen something. He darted into the kitchen. Jerry slithered after him. I turned around. There was Ann, out of uniform, her hair flowing loose.

"I came to say goodbye. Our things are packed," she said. Her eyes moved nervously side to side.

"Packed? Where are you going? What's happening?"

"I can't explain. There isn't enough time. Mick's waiting. We're catching the five o'clock train from Cork."

"You and Mick?" My mind was reeling.

"No!" Ann stepped back. She scowled. "Not that there's anything wrong with Mick. He's been a dear. But she is an entirely different story. You'll hear plenty about what's happened, I'm sure. There's going to be all sorts of talk. Believe half of it—if that much. Trudy isn't all bad. And I'm her friend, no matter what. Look, I really must go. It's been a summer, what?" She leaned forward, gave me a quick hug and was gone.

And she was right. I had only to ask and the 'nods' and 'winks' would wag their tongues. Chef took his sweet time when I came under pressure from the rush of orders at midday meal. He scooped mashed potatoes from the giant pot into a serving dish in exaggerated slow motion.

"Where are the pals? Left you in the lurch?" He smirked and held the dish just out of my reach to make me catch his eye. "Caught out at their own game, huh?"

By word and by deed he was trying to provoke me. By gum and by grace I refused to be baited. When I was ready to ask I knew who could tell me and it certainly wasn't going to be the jilted Chef. Or Timmy-go-fetch. He made a big show cupping his two hands and their dirty black nail beds over his chuckling mouth each time we walked past one another during lunch. And for the first time all summer he hung around during clean up. To Timmy all the trouble was puerile excitement, he wouldn't miss it for anything. Jerry remained aloof which almost seemed like decency but I could give him no credit. He smirked with satisfaction at Chef and Timmy's antics.

Two girls were brought in to help set up and serve dinner that evening. They were from a nearby village. They would be staying a few days, maybe longer, depending on how they worked out. Chef and the lads wasted no time trying to impress them. But these girls were wiser to their ways than the two from England could have been. Besides, the boyos did not press them as much.

After dinner I skipped the singsong and waited outside, hoping Mick Crowley would come to the hotel before going home. But he didn't. Back at her house, Cissy was sitting at the table.

"I waited the tea 'til you'd come," she said.

"Ann said goodbye but told me nothing," I let Cissy know I knew nothing once we settled with cups and bread.

"I have it all."

I knew she would.

"Mick Crowley only just left me. His heart is broken but isn't he the foolish man? I told him weeks ago he'd lost the run of himself, thinking a young one like herself would have any interest in him at all. And she from the city. And from another country. And it England at that," Cissy's incredulity mounted. "What would she be doing anyway, settling down way out the country?" She dismissed the notion.

"She told him as much more than a fortnight ago. But he wouldn't believe it, not until today and she left. 'Twas he drove them to the city. Ann didn't have to leave. It was that other one. The guards finally caught her. She was on young Dineen's boat, a pack of them with her, they all just after coming from the hotel out of their minds with the drink. It wasn't the first time. The guards have been watching her. There were complaints.

"They brought her back to the hotel but the manager wouldn't allow her stay the night. He told Mick to take her to the town, told her never to set foot on hotel grounds again. She told Mick she'd no other choice but to go back to London. She has plenty of money for the journey of course," Cissy put the story to rest on a slur and took a slow sup of tea.

"Ann wouldn't hear of it, your one leaving alone," she added. "Isn't she better off, Ann, I mean? There are ones around here would paint her with the same brush. But she was nothing like that one. Mick Crowley could see that." She took some bread, supped again and held her cup. "It will take him the while but he'll come round."

She placed the cup back in its saucer as if that set everything to right.

A Job

IT WAS HIGH TIME. COUSIN CÁIT said as much three months after Mitch and I married. We were at her kitchen table. Cáit had baked a tart, almond slices and a boiled fruitcake. She stood over the kitchen table and sliced with such vigour even the oozy fruitcake shed crumbs.

"Who's for tea?" Cáit snatched the cosy off the metal pot.

"I'll pour," I offered and reached for the handle.

"What?" Cáit's hand got to it before mine. "You'd only burn yourself." This was Cáit's ritual.

She clutched the handle with her calloused hand and held the pot aloft.

"Cups?" she commanded.

Without stopping their conversation, Mitch and John, Cáit's husband, slid their cups towards her. Cáit winced at the rattle. She poured for them but not for me. Cocking her head she drew her face into a puzzle, put her free hand on her hip and asked, "Why don't you go away and get yourself qualified to do something?"

Cáit had. She ran a playgroup in the converted garage. I dropped by one morning to leave in an angel food cake tin from home. It's for making ring cakes, a deep, heavy, truly non-stick pan. Cáit had never seen the like and wanted to try it out. She leaned it lopsided against the phone on the hall table and told me to come into the garage.

"Children," Cáit clapped her hands. The toddlers looked up from Dinky cars and soft toys. "This is a lady who comes all the way from America," she announced. The three-year-olds stared wide-eyed but unimpressed. "She is going to listen to you while you say your rhymes."

Cáit pointed to a small stool for me and put the toddlers sitting in a bunch on the floor. She directed each child by mouthing the words in exaggerated enunciation. She did not mind mistakes in the actual words so long as there was plenty of expression, the plentier the better. She brooked no shyness, not even in the little girl who kept her head down, eyes to the floor and twisted her fingers while she recited in a voice too small to be heard. Cáit frowned. She led no claps. Only bouncy girls and boys deserved those.

"I want you to say that again and this time you must say it loud enough for us to hear you," she started the shy child off once more. It was too much. After four hesitating lines, the little girl stopped. Tears welled.

"Sit down so," Cáit dismissed her.

When she heard the doorbell ring, mothers coming, the shy girl watched anxiously until hers stepped in. She stood up right away and fastened herself to Mammy's long coat.

"She's coming on grand," Cáit manufactured a smile for the mother. She bent to the child but the child turned away, buried her face.

"So? Tell us," Cáit turned to me now in her steamy kitchen, still withholding the teapot. "What's it you'll do?"

"I'm checking a few things," I assured her. Only one, actually, but Cáit didn't have to know that. She poured for me.

It was Market Research. The bold print in the *Cork Examiner* had caught my eye but sounded highfalutin'. 'No Experience Required' kept me reading. I phoned. She couldn't tell me anything about the work. She was only there to answer the phone. All those inquiring were to come for interview between ten and twelve o'clock on Wednesday.

I found the address on McCurtain Street. It had two numbers. One was still intact. The missing one had left a permanent black rim on the door. It showed up clearly against the faded and chipped paint. The derelict building had once been a small hotel. A faded sign still hung from a rusty metal bar fixed to the wall between the two big first floor windows. At the top of the steps I pushed the heavy door. It was stuck and only stuttered open after I shoved it with all my might.

Inside there was a hand-scrawled notice sellotaped to a door halfway down the hall: 'Interviews'. One hard chair stood against the wall. I sat down, shivered and stiffened. The chair was cold and rickety. I started to think about leaving but then the door to the room opened. A man put his head around, saw me and waved me in. The sleeve of his jacket was short. I followed, left the door ajar and sat across the table. I kept my hands on my lap. Dirty smudges, cracks and gouges scarred the table top.

Keeping his eyes on a sheet of paper, the man asked my name and scribbled it down. He asked if I would be available to work every day the following week and ticked the 'Yes' box. Then he looked up hurriedly, told me where to be Monday morning at ten o'clock and smiled or grimaced, I couldn't tell which but I knew it meant I could go. I had passed the interview.

Monday morning five of us turned up. Jacinta briefed us in the upper room over a corner shop on North Main Street. A British company was about to float a new beer. They wanted to pre-test the market and our job was to carry out tastings and write up a survey.

"We need men," Jacinta arched a pencilled eyebrow and held it. One woman chuckled. The eyebrow relaxed. "Once you have him, bring him up here and sit him across the table," she pointed a painted finger to five sets of chairs paired across five small tables along the walls around the room. "And here's the grilling you'll give him," she spoke in a tone that could put any man in his place and pulled her red lips in a tight grin. She handed us each a clipboard. A questionnaire was snapped under the clamp.

"These are the questions," she pitched her voice high, purposeful. "Three pages. Ask the questions in order, once only, just as you see them written. There's to be no prompting, no conversation. You are to speak distinctly and use your natural tone of voice so that your client feels at ease."

"Allow him enough time to answer but not too much. You are to take down his words exactly as he says them to you. Did you all hear that? We want his exact words. Never mind about his grammar. And it doesn't matter if he doesn't like the lager. The point is to get down his exact words."

"Now, read through the questions for yourselves and see have you any for me," Jacinta lit a cigarette and smoked it artfully. She paced the room while we sat at the tables and carried out our assignment. The questionnaire was clear cut. There was nothing for Jacinta to illuminate.

Getting a man first thing Monday morning was the tricky part. It seemed any man on the street at ten-thirty had an agenda. He was in a rush, late for work, couldn't stop. Or, snapping out the wrist to check the watch, he was dashing to meet a colleague for elevenses. Or he was carrying string-tied parcels for herself, he nodded at the woman moving briskly up the street ten paces ahead. A pair of young men wearing new suits scurried past muttering in conclave. I didn't even try to stop them. They couldn't let up until the white smoke rose. After noon the ties seemed to loosen. From then on our business took on a steady pace.

Jacinta was at the top of the room on a raised platform. She sat at a table she had pulled across the dais, positioning it out of the cold draught that blew up the long, narrow stairway. A two-bar electric heater sat beside her chair toasting her leather knee-high boots.

"Ta," she said each time one of us took a completed questionnaire to her. We stood and waited while she ran the point of her long magenta nail down the pages, checking that all empty spaces were filled in. Then, to protect her nails, she held her fingers so straight they arched backwards and untwisted the screw cap on her fountain pen. Only after she drew a slow tick at the top of the front page of each survey could we go and find our next customer.

Tuesday it rained heavily and poured customers. Word of the free pint had reached the Labour Exchange and a queue formed fast. It trailed halfway up the stairway. We didn't have to go outside at all and none of us even bothered to take a break. It was break enough not having to trudge the stairs and pace the pavement drumming up business. All morning, voices filled the room in a steady, though syncopated, mumble like born-agains speaking in tongues. Suddenly, a little while before lunch, Jacinta scraped back her chair so loud the room stopped. Everyone turned and watched her. She stood up, smoothed down the hips of her narrow skirt, stepped down from her place above us and walked deliberately across the room. Her heavy boots rapped the floor. She clutched the handle on the open door, pulled herself up to her full height and pushed it shut with a bang.

"We don't need any more of that lot," she announced, with some of them sitting right there. "We have enough Cs and Ds. Let them head for their dinners and when the stairs are cleared we'll go after the As and Bs," she walked briskly back to her chair and lit a cigarette.

"What does she mean?" I asked the woman next to me when we broke for lunch.

"Hmm?" she stopped chewing her sandwich and raised her head from the *Examiner*.

"What are As, Bs, Cs and Ds?"

"The categories."

"Of what?"

"Men," she went back to reading, seeming to think that answered me.

I didn't like to intrude again. This was the woman who had overheard my first interview on Monday. I asked my taster which pint he usually drank and read out the choices on the list. His face went blank when I said "Smith-wicks". So I said it again, separating the two syllables even more distinctly: "Smith Wicks". At that, his face spread open in a smile.

"You mean to say, Smithicks?" He said it smoothly and cocked his head at a smart angle. He caught the woman's eye. They had a chummy chuckle. I knew I was bothering her but I wanted to get this category thing straight so I wouldn't goof again.

"Why are there categories?"

"To keep them straight, the *A*s from the *B*s from the *C*s from the *D*s."

I had guessed that much.

"Okay. But what puts the men in which category?"

"Money."

"They pay for a category?"

"They earn for it."

"What do you mean?"

She sighed.

"*A*s a bunch, *B*s do better than most. *C*s get by. *D*s draw the dole," she lifted the paper, spread it wide, blocked me out.

Now I knew. And I didn't like it. Asking a man what work he did, which was the third question on the survey, made me uncomfortable. Knowing it classified him made it somehow worse.

On Wednesday Jacinta prowled around our tables. She hawk-eyed me when one taster took a lot of time. White hair, standing tall, he pulled off his gloves and pressed them together on the table. Next he let his long coat slide off his arms, caught it, folded it in two inside out and smoothed it flat over the back of the chair. He set his scarf and curve-brimmed hat atop with aplomb.

I ignored Jacinta. She wouldn't menace me. Our target was five hundred surveys. I had filled my quota already working fast to keep warm, to keep time passing and to get the job finished. Besides it was Jacinta who'd put the pressure on us in the first place to get the *A*s. If a gentleman had the time to answer, taste and move slowly wasn't he entitled to take it?

"Well, girls," Jacinta considered herself our pal by now, close of business on Wednesday. "We've only forty-seven surveys left to fill," she clapped her hands daintily applauding us.

"That's only nine apiece, sure," the woman next to me had it calculated right away. She would. She was a slacker. She came late each morning, took a longer lunch, extra breaks and got by with it all because she had established her credentials with Jacinta the very first day.

"My sister knows the man runs the business," she told Jacinta. They were at the small table next to mine having a cigarette at break. They shared an ashtray. The woman inched it ever closer to Jacinta's side of the table each time Jacinta tapped ash. "You just say the word. I'll see to it. Your room will be papered before the week's out. And he'll do a deal for you too," she promised.

That wasn't the only bargain Jacinta brokered. It didn't surprise any of us that we finished our full quota on Thursday. A man arrived, walked in looking like a nouveau *A*—blow-dried hair, silk scarf, shoes shone to glisten like patent leather. Not noticing any of us but landing loud on his heel taps so we couldn't help noticing him, he strode directly over to the platform. Jacinta hopped off her chair. They stood together. I was already on my way to return my clipboard and got to Jacinta's table just as the man took an envelope out of the inside pocket of his Abercrombie coat and handed its contents to her. I slipped my board onto the table and couldn't help picking up the gist of their huggermugger.

"Fair play ... beat the deadline ... bonus," he put a tight roll of notes into her flat open hand. She closed her fingers over it, slipped that hand and the other as decoy into her skirt pockets in a show of nonchalance.

"Only four days' work?" Cáit's tone was sharp. It cut through the merit of my week's effort. Resting her wrists on the rim of the baking bowl, she looked me up and down. "Hand me two eggs, could you?" she pointed a floured hand to a dozen in a tray at the end of the counter.

"Four days but we got a whole week's pay," I tried to redeem myself. Cáit took the eggs and got busy about her batter. She didn't bother to reply.

The next week I stopped by the office of a secretarial agency on Oliver Plunkett Street. Right there on the spot the woman in charge gave me a timed typing test. I sat at a table in front of a heavy manual typewriter. Before the timer buzzed I had finished typing the test page.

"Hmm," the woman frowned, puzzled. "We'll do that again, shall we?" She whapped the timer twice, wound it and this time stood over my shoulder. I beat the buzzer again.

"Well done," she beamed. "Where can I reach you?" She walked quickly behind her desk and took a notebook out of the top drawer. She opened it and held her pen ready.

"I'm sorry. The house we're renting is only a year old. It hasn't got a phone. Can I call you?"

"No. It's better if you ring. Make it early, before half-past nine. Have you transport?"

"A bike," I said. It was second-hand, one of the big sturdy

types, heavy, but it made me feel safe negotiating traffic. With Cork's hills I got off and pushed a lot anyway.

"A skirt?" she looked at my jeans. Girls did not wear them in Cork then but with the constant wind, jeans made sense on a bike.

"For work? Sure," I assured her.

Two mornings later I rang in expecting to arrange something for the next week. It was lashing rain. I bent double against the wind walking to the telephone kiosk. It was six blocks from the house. Huddling inside didn't give much protection. The door banged at every gust of wind. I dialled and waited. No-one answered. I checked my watch. It was twenty after nine. The woman had said to call before half past. So I dialled again. Still no answer. I stepped lightly from foot to foot trying to keep warm while I waited. Fifteen minutes and six dials later the woman at the agency answered. I heard her flick through pages.

"Can you be on Wellington Road by ten o'clock?" she asked.

I checked my watch, twenty to ten. It would take ten minutes to walk home, pack up dry tights and shoes and get my bike. It would be another half hour biking across town and then I might need more time to locate the place.

"Would ten-thirty be alright?" I shaved it close.

"The man at the firm said ten o'clock. He was quite adamant," she told me.

"I'm sorry. But I just can't make it by then."

"Not to worry. I can phone one of our regular girls," she said and left me listening to the dial tone.

Maybe I should have lied, arrived late and made up an excuse. Or maybe, I thought as I trudged home in puddles, I don't need this. Like most kids I had taken a typing course the summer after freshman year in high school. Typing came in handy for essays and working on school publications. It helped you get a summer job. I had worked for an insurance company filing up claim forms two summers in a row. Typing was a useful skill, not career leverage. Besides I had gotten a letter in the post calling me to an interview. A pre-school playgroup was being set up in a block of flats in Blackpool. They were looking for someone to run it.

"I know the nuns. I had a coffee morning for one of their shelters," Cáit told me two nights later when Mitch and I called in. "I'll put in a word."

"Don't," I said urgently. "The letter said no canvassing. I'll be disqualified."

"Don't be daft. Sure you'll get nowhere without the bit of pull." Cáit took her hands out of the dishwater and picked up a towel. "I'm telling you," came the usual preface to the wisest of her thoughts, "they're all doing it. It's not what you know but who you contact."

"I'm an outsider ... " I started to explain my perspective.

"Exactly! But there are ways around that too."

"No there aren't. And if I try any tricks, they're only going to backfire."

"But it's I who have the contacts," Cáit protested like I was trying to steal the march.

"I know. That's just the point. I'm the one applying for the job. It's up to me."

"Would you listen to this?" Cáit rounded on Mitch and John, just coming into the kitchen for supper. In her own words she repeated mine using a tone that highlighted the nonsense of my view.

"Where's this place?" John asked Cáit, ignoring me. She told him.

"Isn't that Ned Sullivan's constituency?" he asked Mitch. Mitch nodded.

"Don't you know him from the college? Couldn't you give him a ring?" John prodded Mitch.

"Of course he will. While I'll have a word with Sister," Cáit plugged in the kettle and filled the pot. "Take down the cups, will you?" she directed me.

"No," I said. Six eyes riveted on me. "I really wish you wouldn't. I want the interview to be straight, no hidden agenda."

"Do you want this job or don't you?" John asked and went on, "I presume you do. Why else did you apply for it? In that case, what's the harm, if we have the contacts? They might do you a good turn."

"I don't want a turn. I want a fair chance."

"Ha!" John scoffed. "Wouldn't it be just grand if life could be so simple?" he talked to Mitch but for my benefit.

Pulling a cup and plate over to himself he pointed at the spoons. I handed him one. He took it without looking at me. Cáit came, sliced and poured.

"Do you know," she said looking past me to somewhere in her mind, "when I was starting out with the playgroup I hadn't a clue how to go about it? I thought all I had to do was make out a few notices and put them around in the shops and the mothers would see them and I'd have my playgroup. So I did just that and sat back and waited. And I'll tell you this much," she looked at John as if he'd never heard the story, not to mind lived through it. He quickly darted his eyes on and off me to see was I paying attention. "I could be sitting at the phone to this very day. It never rang. There wasn't a tattle out of it. Nothing happened, not until I took the advice of a neighbour, an older woman. We only knew each other to see. But a week after my notices were up she called to the door. She told me her daughter had two children and she might be interested in sending them to a playgroup. 'Have you places left?' she asked me. So I told her. I admitted it. 'Not one single enquiry has come in,' I said it straight out. It was then she gave me her advice. More tea?" Cáit stopped for effect. John pointed to his cup for a hot drop. I shook my head. I'd had enough. Cáit went on.

"'Have you said it around?' this woman asked me. 'For no-one takes the time with notices. And even if they do the details go right out of their heads. It's word of mouth will get you going.'

"And do you know this much? I hadn't," Cáit raised her right hand and clicked her fingers in the air, "that much confidence. Had I, John?" John blinked. "But I made myself get out and away from that telephone. I went up to women, talked to them, let them know what I was up to. And sure, weren't they only delighted. Within the fortnight I had my ten. And all because,"—she put her eyes on me. I could have recited but didn't—"I took my neighbour's advice."

"Amazing," I said and buttered a slice of spotted dog I didn't want. I cut it down the middle, handed Mitch half and slipped him the eye to go soon.

There were three people on the interview panel for the new playschool, a social worker, a Sister and a man from the Corporation. They sat in a line behind a table on straight-backed chairs in a dim room lit by a ceiling light that dispelled only a small circle of greyness around it. Thin curtains of no colour hung lankly over small windows high up one wall. I could see rust on the metal frames through the skimpy fabric that stuck in places to the windows weeping with condensation. A filing cabinet stood out so starkly from a corner behind the table it seemed intimidating. A two-bar electric heater crouched low on the grey carpet tiles beside the cabinet. There was no office equipment. It was impossible to tell whether this was a permanent or temporary place on the ground floor of the block of flats.

The man extended his hand towards the chair across the table. I lifted it out and sat. My letter of application was in front of them. They took it in turns to ask me questions. Sister wanted to know about the volunteer work I had done for two years in university.

"I tutored slow learners twice a week in a primary school off campus. It was after school for about an hour. They were seven and eight years old. Reading was usually the problem, sometimes arithmetic, simple addition and subtraction."

"And what training did you have?" she asked.

"None," I admitted point-blank. "The teacher set out the material and she kept an eye on how we were doing. These were kids whose parents couldn't put in the extra time. That's what I did."

Sister made no comment. I saw no reaction in her eyes. She kept her face immobile.

"What brought you to Cork?" she asked.

"I came to study for a year. And then came back a year later to get married. Mitch is from Cork," I told her. It crossed my mind that this might be an innings, make me less an outsider.

"How long do you intend staying?"

The question took me aback. I'd never thought about it, didn't have to. Marriage means forever. Or was Sister implying something, something to do with America and divorce? I looked at her but her face gave nothing away.

"I'm here for good," I said.

The social worker was next. She looked only a little bit older than I was, so I expected an easier rapport. But there wasn't one. She looked me in the eye. She did not smile.

"Your only work with pre-school children was," she ran her eyes up and down my application—I felt certain she had this all played out, the way she went straight at me in a negative vein without preamble—"when you were in high school, what we call secondary school?"

"That's right."

"And?" she asked pertly.

"On Saturdays I went to a day centre and helped out, playing with the kids."

"Just playing with the children?" She stressed 'children'.

"Yes. But it wasn't 'just playing'. There was more to it. The kids at the centre didn't take to a stranger right away. They were even wary of a teenager—slow to like you. They'd had a tough time and it showed. Some of them wouldn't look at you or take your hand or talk, not for a long time."

"Did you have any training?"

"No."

"Was your work evaluated?"

"Not in a formal way. But the director and I always talked after the kids went home. She wanted to hear what I saw, the things I noticed. She listened carefully. After a while the kids opened up. They weren't afraid to be spontaneous. We had some real fun. There was warmth between us."

"But there was never an evaluation," she went back to the negative to make sure we ended there. I felt like I'd walked into a trap and couldn't tell whether it was because she had something against me or had someone else in mind for the job.

"How long did you say you're in Cork?" It was the man's turn.

"Six months for good. But there was the year in UCC."

"And do you know many people yet?" he asked.

"I'm beginning to," I said.

"Would you know anyone, say, in an official capacity?"

"Pardon me?"

"Do you know anyone who holds public office?"

"Yes."

"And did you contact him about this job?"

"No," I said and decided to come clean. I had nothing to hide. "I've met Ned Sullivan. Friends told me I should go to him, tell him I'd applied. When I wouldn't, they told me I was daft."

"I see," he said. His voice was wooden, his face blank. There was no telling what he saw.

The interview ended with a few courtesies. It was a relief to get outside. The wind was driving the rain. It belted me and it felt good. Out in the open I knew what I was up against. I pedalled hard to drive out the frustration. I knew I wouldn't get the job which didn't bother me so much. The interview did. There was something behind their questions. My answers were direct, clear, without ramification. Yet, the panel had culled some things. They'd weighed me up, taken my measure. I felt I'd disclosed far more than my words intended.

"I can't tell you. I've no idea," I told Cáit when she asked me how the interview went. Her voice was blasé but I could hear the curiosity. I wasn't going to feed it with the details.

We were at her house, out in front. I'd biked over to give her slips from a philodendron and the offspring from a spider plant. I'd promised them to her when she had admired the plants. I stayed on my bike on purpose, didn't want to be drawn into the kitchen.

"When will you hear from them?" she asked.

"I won't," I said.

"What makes you say that?"

"I can tell," I said and started to turn my bike to leave.

"In that case, I can tell you," she said quickly.

"Tell me what?" I leaned back against the seat.

"I had a word with Sister, not the Sister on the interview board, my Sister. And it wasn't until after the interview. She told me you did a great one. She said it's a pity they can't hire two leaders for the playgroup. She said you'd make a fine assistant," Cáit touched my arm and fixed me with a steady smile, the same one she manufactured for the shy child's mother. "Come in. We'll put on the kettle."

"Sorry, Cáit. I can't. I have some errands to run."

I turned the wheel of my bike, spun the pedal into place and pushed off. Biking down the street I picked up good speed. The wind was at my back. Rounding the corner I looked over my shoulder. So was Cáit.

Christmas

"SORRY TO KEEP YOU," MISS BROCKIE said, or something like it. She was missing a number of teeth and spoke through the gaps.

"It's okay," I smiled and didn't know where to look. Her eyes swam in a blur behind thick glasses. I couldn't see the pupils clearly, couldn't begin to read her. "I hope I'm not disturbing you?" I nodded down the counter referring to her coterie standing there in a cluster.

"Not a bit," Miss Brockie did a quarter turn away from me and looked over her shoulder. She was checking the door to the living quarters. Mrs. Sheehan, the proprietress, kept it open when she put Miss Brockie in charge of the shop.

"You had your's made long 'go," Miss Brockie turned back to me.

"Huh-uh. Not me," I had to admit.

"How so?" she asked. "I thought you Yanks were always quick with the Christmas."

"Maybe we are but I've never heard of plum pudding and

I don't bake fruitcakes." I couldn't admit I didn't know how. Her friends would batter me with instructions. "We bake cookies," I answered. Miss Brockie's face scrunched up quizzically at me.

I described the cookies—shortbread with whole pecans, sugar dough cut into Christmas shapes, a crumbly mixture moistened with whiskey—"and Daddy made walnut fudge from a recipe he keeps hidden where none of us will ever find it."

"In his head," Miss Brockie said.

"How'd you know that?"

"Ah-ha!" she tapped her temple where the invisible hairnet met her skin.

Miss Brockie was in the know of a lot of things. Her inscrutable face invited conversation, even disclosure. In spite of the damp chill that the three-bar electric heater never dispelled, when Miss Brockie was behind the counter the shop was a snug. Women stayed so long I couldn't see when they ever got around to the housework and messages and other people's business they gave out about.

"What can I get for you?" Miss Brockie asked me.

"Oh. Yeah." Conversation made it easy to forget I came for something. "Could I have," the list came to me slowly, "a loaf of brown bread, a pint of milk, some red cheddar cheese and a quarter pound of ham, please? Oh. And a half dozen eggs. You've put me in the mood to bake."

While Miss Brockie got the things together I leaned sideways to listen. The women were talking plum pudding.

"Suet's your man for the texture."

"Suet? Himself wouldn't have it."

"Himself is it? And how would he know?"

"Porter's the trick," a voice interjected.

"And a dash of the cr'ature."

"If you can get the real thing," a knowing voice added and lowered itself. The heads huddled. "Con-the-post brings mine. He's a sister in the country, but I won't say where. She ferments specially for the season. I give both the cake and the pud a good dash and keep it up with the cake every Tuesday in November. Before I go to the bingo I take it from the tin, fold down the greaseproof paper and give the cake a good spiking. A knitting needle's handy out. Number eleven goes right the way through. It's then I pour in the pure 'til each spike is filled to the brim. Come the day, the cake is soaked gorgeous," she gave a proud shift to her shoulders and settled them under her coat.

"I'll only ever use brandy," tolled a voice that put an end to the discussion on a note far higher than most would aspire.

"That's one pound and six pence," Miss Brockie drew a line across the brown paper bag where she'd totted up the figures. The paper was slick. She pressed her knobby pencil hard. It scratched, made me shiver.

"He'll be wanting his cake, won't he?" I knew Miss Brockie was referring to Mitch. She always found a way to.

"Our wedding cake's still fresh. I kept a wedge stored way back in the coldest corner of a kitchen cabinet."

"Right so," she nodded.

Mitch and I would be alone anyway. Our friends all had family to go to which made things hard for me. I was trying not to get uneasy about this first Christmas in a new place but couldn't keep my mind from drifting back home, as it did now when I walked away from the shop. It was dark at four thirty. The wind had died down. The rain was a light drizzle but heavy enough to bring down the smoke coming up out of every chimney I passed. The smell of turf smugged the air.

It was Monday, December 20th. They'd have gotten the tree yesterday. We always went for it the last Sunday before Christmas, loading up the station wagon with ropes, saws, clippers and sleds, if there was snow on the ground. The boys brought Spot to give him a good run. Along the highway outside the city limits Daddy slowed down when we passed any woods. He was looking for the greenest clump of cedar trees. Mile after mile he kept searching.

"There are some real pretty ones over there," Mom might point out to speed things up.

But Daddy had to choose the spot himself, like he had found the exact picture in a dream or a memory.

"There it is!" he'd cry out at last, then turn off the highway onto a side road and into a long, dirt drive up to a farmer's house to ask permission to go across the field and into the woods to cut a tree. No one ever said no but one year Daddy didn't get to ask. Before he could switch off the engine, the farmer's dog ran out of the open barn door. He spied Spot and growled deeply outside my door. Then he sprang forward barking madly. Spot clawed my legs, his drool dripped on my hand as he clambered to the window to bark back.

"God dang dogs," Daddy shook his jowls and shifted into reverse. "Why don't they bring their 'leash law' out here and quit trying to tie up every dog living in town?"

"Dogs don't cause trouble out here. There aren't as many cars to chase in the country," Mom pointed out but her logic made matters worse.

"What do you call this?" Daddy lifted his hands and whacked the steering wheel. "I can't even get out of my car!" Spot gave a sharp bark like he understood and was voting 'No' to the new leash law. Daddy went silent then, Spot too, but he didn't quit panting until Daddy found and negotiated a new neck of the woods.

"It's Christmas!" Mom tried to jolly Daddy out of his sulk while we unpacked the car. "Let's forget the dogs and find a tree."

Spot must've understood that too. At the word 'tree' he scrambled over the middle and third seats, jumped out of the tailgate and ran to a nearby dogwood tree. He looked up at its branches. There must have been a squirrel.

Like every other year we walked a long time before Daddy divined just the right tree, full bodied for him, with clusters of blue cedar berries for Mom. The berries kept the cedar aroma wafting through the house all through Christmas. It was heavy work dragging the tree over brittle field stubble, sometimes a creek, always a steep hill. Back at the road Daddy and the boys hoisted the tree onto the luggage rack and criss-crossed it into place with rope.

I wondered now who took my job this year, putting the lights on the tree. I always set them deep in the branches so the tree would glow from within, not shine like tinsel town. Homesick, needing ritual, I went to Miss Brockie the next morning.

"Where can I find some holly?" I asked her.

"We don't sell it but they do down the Coal Quay," she told me.

"No. I want to cut some," I said.

Miss Brockie stared down at the *Cork Examiner* she had spread out on the counter. After a little while she glanced over her shoulder and then moved down the counter. She came out from behind it and, with a quick lift of her chin, beckoned me to come close.

"Go out the long road," I leaned down so I could hear her whisper. "At the T-junction you'll see a field to your left. Go beyond the gate 'til you'll come to a small opening in the hedge, then through it, up along to the top—there's where you'll find your holly." She plucked a broom standing in the corner and walked to the front door. I opened it. She ducked out under my arm.

"You're not to let on 'twas I told you if you're asked," she warned me.

"I won't," I promised and skipped out of the way. She was swiping the doormat with all her might.

I found the landmarks just as Miss Brockie directed only it wasn't easy going. At the hedge opening the tufted embankment was more growth than ground. My foot slipped, slapped and sank into a rill running under the overgrown grasses. My desert boot got stuck, wedged into the width of the runnel.

I stooped and tugged my ankle. The wind whipped my hair into a tangle of briars and held me bent double. I fingered the clump of hair and unsnagged most but some got caught like sheep's wool on barbed wire. Forensics could trace me now if picking holly were against the law. There was something fishy, after all, from the way Miss Brockie acted. I wriggled up some movement in my foot and freed it then burrowed through the hedge on all fours and stood up to see, in the far corner as Miss Brockie had said, three pot-bellied holly bushes bulging with berries. I snapped small shoots from each bush so as not to distort their natural shapes and put each sprig into the plastic bag I'd scrunched into my pocket. Before going home I took my bundle straight to the shop.

"Do you want some?" I held the bag up and open for Miss Brockie to see.

"One will do," she took a sprig without looking and slipped it into the pocket of her blue duster. Ouch! Her face contorted. A thorny leaf had scratched her.

"Are you okay?" I asked.

Miss Brockie dabbed the hand and slipped her hanky back up the sleeve.

She ignored my concern, asked me nothing about the holly.

"What can I get you?" she raised her chin in imitation of a real shopkeeper.

"Nothing. I was just here this morning," I reminded her.

"Right so," she bent her head back to the *Examiner*.

If holly didn't matter to Miss Brockie, I'd make it matter to Mitch. When I got home I wriggled wire through the holly and twisted it tight to hold the sturdy twigs in a wreath. I secured the wreath to the front door knocker and went to the kitchen to tend my hands. They were scored with cuts much worse than Missouri cedar scratches. I rubbed in ointment and switched on the light over the doorstep. That way Mitch would see the wreath first thing.

"It has to come down," Mitch was matter-of-fact.

"Oh, don't worry. It's secure. The wind can't move it. It won't scratch the paint," I assured him. Why else could he want it down?

"Have you seen wreaths on any other doors?" he asked me.

"Not yet. But what's ever on time here?"

"We don't hang wreaths on doors ... " he started. Mitch could be long-winded. I cut in.

"That's not going to stop me." I was doing my best to conjure a Christmas. Being different was not going to hold me back. Ireland wasn't the only country with traditions.

"You don't understand."

No, I didn't.

"Wreaths are normally associated with death and funerals," he looked me in the eye and stared the point home.

I didn't like to, but took down the wreath and hung it on the kitchen door. Just in time. Cousin Cáit came by, a first. She'd told me she made it a rule: "I never call to anyone during the first year they are married, not unless I am specifically invited. That way I'm certain I'll not embarrass myself by calling at the wrong time," she added and gave me a pointed look as if I hadn't gotten the drift. But the blank look on my face wasn't because I didn't know what she was getting at. I couldn't believe she actually meant it.

"I'm badly stuck," came her next declaration. "Can you sing?" she stayed standing in the hallway, didn't have time to sit.

"I'm okay in a group."

"Just the thing. It's people I need, doesn't matter about the voice. Christmas Eve, on Patrick Street, outside The Moderne, do you know it?" I nodded yes. She didn't see me nod, went ahead without catching breath. "They do women's fashion. It's right there, next to Dunnes Stores. It's only a few old carols we'll be singing. I'm sure you'll know them. You're to be there at three. We're collecting for the hospice."

With that she left, taking for granted I would turn up.

I carolled a lot when I was growing up. A friend's sister had cerebral palsy and we sang door to door collecting for her clinic. Most houses expected us, many invited us in for hot chocolate and cookies. At one or two houses, however, we stood and sang 'til we were hoarse but no-one came to the door even though we could see their shadows when we peeked through cracks in their curtains. We gave these houses fair warning—one, two, three times we pressed the doorbell, stopping singing to make sure it rang. When they still didn't answer we twisted the bulbs on their outdoor decorations just far enough to put out the light. Our gloves slipped on the slick bulbs but we managed. It would be fun to carol again.

Heavy drizzle hung over Cork Christmas Eve morning. By afternoon a cold breeze had developed. It wasn't strong enough to disperse or lift the clouds. Even before I turned the corner at the end of our block on my way to town, dampness permeated the extra layers of clothes I had put on. Twelve of us turned up.

"Let you bigger ones stand at the back," Cáit lined us up in two rows. "Take that instrument to the back," she told a tall, thin schoolgirl holding a tin whistle. Head bent, the girl obeyed. "Shove in, you," Cáit told me, to make room for the schoolgirl.

"Stand here, pet, out the front. And you're to hold this," Cáit handed Tin Whistle's younger brother a wicker basket. He took the handle and held the basket down at his side. Cáit grabbed his wrist, stretched his arm straight out to the front and parked it in mid-air. "The basket must be seen," she told him and let go of his arm. It dropped back to his side. Cáit scowled. "Right so. But when anyone goes to put in some coins, mind you lift the basket out to them. It's you'll be crawling after coins that fall to the ground," she warned the boy.

"Has everyone a copy of the carols?"

We nodded.

"We'll begin then, 'Jingle Bells' to warm us up. I'm sure ye all know it. Don't let me see any of ye bending your faces to read the words. Ye'll only constrict your throats. Ye must sing out. We must be heard if we want to attract attention. And take no notice of the tin whistle. Don't let her playing throw any of ye," she smiled big at the girl by my side. I could feel the girl squirm. Then counting, one and a two and a ... "Dashing through the snow in a ... " Cáit swivelled to face front. Hand aloft she beat time until we caught up with her. Some voices, past their prime, quivered. A couple were loud and assured. Tin Whistle blew in runs and bleeps. Standing so close I could not tell whether I was in or out of key but I kept pace with the words. They, at least, are the same the world over.

Town was packed. Shoppers charged regardless of anything or anyone else. We crammed back to give them space but two rows deep took up a lot of sidewalk. We got jostled by the crowds. Still, many people stopped, dug coins from pockets or purses and made hasty contributions. Cáit, her strong soprano never missing a note, acknowledged each with a large, formal nod.

Traffic grew heavy. Tyres hissed over the rain accumulating on the streets and wipers slapped across windshields stopped at the traffic lights just up from where we stood. We strained our voices to be heard. Into the second hour my lips and legs stiffened from the cold. I shifted foot to foot, did toe stands and alternately fisted and splayed my gloved fingers to work up circulation. I had never been so cold, not even when I carolled in snow two feet deep, temperature near freezing and both still falling.

"Look at you. You've turned blue," Cáit scolded when at long last the carolling was over.

"I'm okay," my tight face gave me a robot's jaw and the stiff grin of a ventriloquist.

"Your lips are purple!" she said in a tone that made it my fault. "Do you need a lift?" She looked at me like I was pathetic.

"I'n 'eeting 'itch ... " I managed to say.

Cáit understood or hadn't listened. She cut me off before I could go on to tell her Mitch wasn't coming for another hour.

"Right so. How are ye fixed for tomorrow? Will ye come to us or what?"

Truth told it was too late to accept her invitation even though I had hoped, even half expected she'd ask us over for Christmas dinner. The waiting had corroded the desire. Coming now, only after I'd turned up to sing, the invitation didn't seem genuine. Besides, I had gotten fresh food at the grocery store that morning.

"No thanks. I have things to cook," I chose words for my tight lips.

"You'll come for your tea, so," Cáit said and left before I could answer.

On my way to City Hall to meet Mitch I passed the main post office on Oliver Plunkett and then turned down a connecting street to get to the South Mall. I looked in the open door of a fruit and flower shop. Out the back in a storage area I saw a few Christmas trees flopped against the wall and on the floor. I went through to the back. A young man in a black plastic anorak was bending, lifting and piling empty wooden crates.

"Excuse me. Are the trees still for sale?" I asked his back.

My jaws were working again. I'd browsed through Roches to warm up.

"A pound a piece," he told me without turning or breaking the rhythm of his stacking.

I pulled off a glove and checked my coat pocket.

"Will this do?" I held out my hand.

He stopped, straightened up and turned to me. Both our heads bowed to my hand. We counted the coins and looked up in sync. Our eyes met.

"You must be joking," he said.

I gave him a look, not pleading, just doleful. "It's Christmas Eve, ten to five," I prompted and edged my open hand out further, offering all I had.

"Huh!" he exhaled a smirk. "Take one so. They're not much good to me now anyway," he turned back to his work. The sleeves of his anorak whispered against its body.

"Here," I stepped forward and put my open hand almost under his chin. He stopped, put his hands on his hips, sighed, rolled his eyes and chortled as he took the two shillings and sixpence.

I turned and picked up the tree nearest me. I stood it, a sparse-limbed pine, at arm's length, looked it over and gave it a sharp shake. Needles rained down—a 'shedder'. Lifting it with one hand I turned to leave.

"Merry Christmas," I said. Then remembered it's 'happy'.

"And you," he said too busy finishing up to look at me and see he'd made my day. His offhand generosity and having my first Christmas tree in Ireland lifted the sopping sky that hung over me. I shivvied along the South Mall, onto Parnell Bridge and crossed over at the Model School to City Hall and stood at our agreed meeting place. I parked the tree against the iron railing and kept a lookout for Mitch. When I waved he negotiated the car to the kerbside. I opened the passenger door and bent in.

"Look what I got," I threw my arm out towards the tree.

"What?" Mitch was preoccupied watching traffic through the rear-view mirror.

"The tree! Right there!" I left the car and brought it over. I opened the back door and started to put the tree in, base first to protect the branches.

"It won't fit," Mitch raised his shoulder and ducked so the needles wouldn't scratch his face.

"I bet it will," I raised the top of the tree and laid it over the front passenger seat.

"And I bet you'll be walking."

"There," I shut the back door with a bang and got in the front seat.

"What's this all about?" Mitch talked through the branches that fell between us.

"Guess, Mitch. Go on. Give it a try. Why do you think I would stand in the rain singing for two hours, then buy a pine tree, carry it ten blocks and heave it unaided into the car on December twenty-fourth?" I parted the branches and smiled to lighten my sarcasm.

"Where are you going to put it? How will you stand it up?" Mitch swerved adroitly into traffic and just as deftly tried to insinuate the work onto me.

"By the fire. In a bucket. We'll manage."

We didn't have tree lights so nothing had to be plugged in and the tree didn't have to hug the wall. We stood it right in the centre of the room away from the fireplace. Mitch held it upright in the scrubbing bucket while I ran in and out the front door scraping up and carrying handfuls of gravel from the front drive. It took seventeen trips to fill the bucket so it held the tree steady.

To decorate it I opened out and carefully balanced any bright Christmas cards we'd gotten on the sturdy lower branches. On the top branches I hung four delicate ornaments Mom had sent wrapped in layers of tissue paper in our Christmas box. I hooked them on the fire side so when I tapped them they would spin and scatter the reflected firelight. Just before closing we walked to the shop. Miss Brockie was so absorbed in the *Evening Echo* she didn't hear us come in.

"Happy Christmas," I slipped a tin of cookies I had baked onto the counter on the edge of the paper.

"Jesus, Mary and Joseph!" Miss Brockie jumped back and clapped a hand over her mouth, too late. "Would you listen to the language," she took her hand away.

"It isn't blasphemy at all, Miss Brockie but a most appropriate greeting given the night that it is," Mitch told her.

"So 'tis," Miss Brockie readily took his absolution and laughed in the girlish way she always did for Mitch. Looking up at him she overlooked my tin.

"Have you got any plans for tomorrow?" I asked.

"I always go to my sister. She has the brother and myself and all her own crowd too. There's four grandchildren now. I'll be going early to give a hand and then I'll stop the night. She wants me to stay longer but I'm due back here the day after Stephen's Day."

"Mind yourself. Take it easy on the pudding. And don't let us be hearing any rumours about you with the brandy," Mitch set her skittish again.

"Go 'way with yourself," she shooed him with her hand and then let it fall to the counter. Her fingers brushed my tin. Good. She would know it was there.

"Enjoy your celebrations," I said.

"And yourselves," she responded with a smile that followed Mitch out the door.

Christmas Mass was crowded, long and distracting. Extras appeared in the choir. Children brought Santa gifts. Mothers tried to stop them playing. The mikes were turned up so the priest's voice boomed. It wasn't the stillness of Bethlehem but it was celebration.

Mitch and I ate the chicken fillets I had marinated with steamed broccoli and twice-baked potatoes. Cáit would have flaky pastry tarts and lashings of cream so we didn't have dessert. Except Mitch surprised me. He'd bought a Battenberg from Thompson's bakery, his favourite. After we ate, Mitch read and I set to the *New York Times* Christmas crossword. It was syndicated throughout the US. Many local papers published it. Mom had sent the Christmas one, published in advance. At university I had grown addicted, adept at its quirks and humours. But today the clues were abstruse which surprised me. The Christmas clues were normally made easier. Had I lost the knack or was I out of touch or both?

"Let's go," I dropped the crossword onto the floor. Trying to tease it out was making me restive.

"Is it time?" Mitch asked.

"Time doesn't matter on Christmas," I said.

But it did. I was fighting it since I woke. They were six hours behind at home. I wouldn't be able to put Christmas to bed until far into the night.

John came to the door.

"Cáit's in bed. I don't know where the children are, off upstairs or out the back with the bits and pieces Santie brought," he put our coats on the newel post and took us to the sitting room.

"We bring the television in here for Christmas in case there's anything worth looking at. I'm watching some old farce of an effort. The gags are flat and you'd want to be working for RTE to get a laugh out of the jokes. They're only meant for the in-crowd up there in Donnybrook," he dismissed the variety show. "I'm waiting for Peggy Dell to come on. What'll you have?"

John poured a whiskey for Mitch and himself. I didn't take anything, didn't want to add alcohol to a tummy rumbling with lonesomeness. We talked over the volume of the television. John kept an eye on its shenanigans.

"Whisht," he stopped Mitch mid-sentence. Peggy Dell was on. She was low-key and had a barely withheld sass. Her fingers sidled across the piano keys coaxing out a syncopated accompaniment to her low-slung voice. She was a blessed counterpoise to the forced jollity that had gone before, reminded me, in fact, of my great-uncle. He'd have loved her. He'd be at our house about now, along with the others. My great-aunts and my grandmother always sat together talking in ladylike whispers while the men stood and vied, one story topping another.

Calvin Monroe Hill, Uncle Pug for short, came dressed up in a cream linen suit, starched white shirt, bow tie and two-toned Oxford shoes. He looked fit to kill and the aunts looked ready to pull the trigger. Pug's voice cracked like a shot when he told his untoward tales. The aunts put their white hands to hushing their mouths. Unabashed, Pug inhaled his cigar or took a swig of his highball and stared straight-eyed down through his bifocals at the aunts which set them tut-tutting behind their hands. Their shame-on-you was feigned. I could see their eyes dance, delighted to be indignant.

"It's here you are," Cáit was in the room in a burst.

"Cáit!" I was startled. "You're not sick?"

"What?" A ridge burrowed between her eyebrows.

"I thought you might've caught cold or something yesterday and that's why you were in bed."

"Not at all, girl. I was only taking a lie down. You'd need one after serving up a meal to this crowd," she rolled her eyes at John. I was glad we hadn't added to her burden. "Come to the kitchen. We'll make the tea."

Cáit swung into action. I fetched when asked but otherwise did not get in her way. In no time she had a tray weighed down with turkey sandwiches, Christmas cake, mince tartlets and the pudding.

"Catch the door for me there," Cáit directed. She carried the tray past me into the hallway. I slithered around her, keeping my grip on the teapot steady, and held open the door to the sitting room. Cáit entered like one of the Magi.

The three kids were called, the couch pulled back and chairs pulled in so everyone had a place to sit. John and Cáit and Mitch told stories from growing up in the village which, it became apparent, had been like an extended family. It was foreign to me. I could only listen, nothing I could tell would have fitted in. Maybe someday my stories would matter. We stayed quite late. By the time we left, Christmas was over on both sides of the Atlantic.

A few days later Mitch and I ran out of coffee. I didn't want to buy a new jar. Mitch seldom drank it and I had made half a New Year's resolution to get off it by cutting down to one cup a day. But half a resolution is as good as none and there's always Lent, so around noon I went to Miss Brockie.

"They liked the cookies," she said, rhyming it with 'fluke' as soon as I stepped up to the counter. "I told them a real Yank was after baking them and that's why the ones with nuts were different."

"Oh?" Good different or bad different?

"They thought I was after selling you something special to put into them. I said no, it had nothing to do with me at all. They said I was trying to keep it a secret. 'And how,' I asked, 'could I keep anything in that shop a secret? Can't you see for yourselves everything that's on the shelves?' 'It's what passes under the counter that counts,' says my sister's husband. I rounded on him, told him not to be commenting. The cheek of him, putting me in a low light. I wouldn't dream of doing that class of a thing." She raised herself on tiptoe, leaned up over the counter and lowered her voice. I bent in.

"And even if I was to be tempted, how could I get away with anything in here and herself," she flicked her head at the door opened to the inner sanctum, "right inside and her ear cocked to me?" She pulled back down to her natural height and chuckled at her audacity—whispering about Mrs. Sheehan right in front of her back.

"You want to know what I put in the cookies?" I asked.

"I do. Weren't they the first to disappear?"

I stalled to relish the moment. Disclosure was in my court

for the first time ever. Looking first to my left, then to my right, I whispered, "hickory nuts."

Miss Brockie frowned.

"And where do you come across them, tell me?"

"They grow in Missouri. My Dad gets a bag every year and shells them for Christmas."

"Say the name again for me?"

"Hickory, like in ... "

"Dickory dock," Miss Brockie beamed.

"Do you have any coffee? The instant kind?" I asked. Not every shop sold jars then.

"You'll have to give me a minute 'til I'll climb to the upper shelves. There's not many asks for it."

She went to the ladder, three times her height, and ran it along the shelves. Over at the window I picked up the *Examiner* and the *Times* and went down the row reading front page headlines. Miss Brockie was still on the ladder. I watched her pull a small jar out through two rungs and then, hugging her arms around the ladder, she pulled her sleeve over her wrist and dusted off the lid. Looking further up, curious to know what other commodities were not in demand, I saw it, there at the very top, secured to the left support of the ladder—my sprig of holly. Miss Brockie climbed down, sure-footed as a crab on the ocean floor.

"I see you're left-handed," I thought I could put one past her.

She paused to think a second. Her head twitched upwards, on target, right at the holly. "So I am. But I don't let the right one know what the left one's getting up to," she said, making a point. There was some veiled meaning but my quickest twists of mind couldn't be up to it.

"So what did your left hand do with the holly that your right hand shouldn't know?" I asked outright.

Her finger flew to her lips. We huddled again.

"I put the holly up high there where herself wouldn't have a close view of it. The way she keeps her eye on every ha' penny goes in and out the till, I know she'd recognise it, even that bit of a piece."

"Recognise holly?" Was this nonsense?

"'Tis she that owns the fields," Miss Brockie stood back up, straightened her shoulders and continued, "but I won't be removing it until 'tis time." She spoke like someone was trying to make her.

"Time for what?"

"When the Christmas is over."

"But it is over, more than a week ago now."

"Is that the way the Yanks see it?"

"Miss Brockie," I addressed her by name keeping one thing straight at least. "We're three days into the New Year. Today is January third. Christmas was December twenty-fifth. To me, Yank or not, that means it's over."

"Ah, but you're forgetting," she smiled 'cos she had me here.

"Forgetting what?" I kept exasperation out of my voice. Miss Brockie pushed the coffee and a small carton of cream into a brown bag so small it would split from the strain if anyone less skilful had bagged it so tightly.

"You forget there's women's Christmas."

"What? What's women's Christmas?"

"Some would call it 'little' but 'tis all the same."

"But what is it?"

"It's January sixth, sure," she said like only a fool did not know.

"The Epiphany?"

"The same," she seemed satisfied. I wasn't.

"But why's it called 'women's'? The Magi were men." I could see no reason.

"It's the day the men do the women's work. The men are meant to make the dinner and if they don't know how, and I'd say there's a fair few that haven't a clue, they're to take the women out for a meal. It's for all the work the women are after putting into the Christmas."

"Do men know about it?" Mitch had never said anything, he who knew all about wreaths.

"Not that they'd let on or take much notice if the women didn't remind them."

"I see," I rustled my messages into the crook of my arm and paid.

"So you tell himself he's to look after the dinner the day," Miss Brockie handed me the change.

"May I say you said so?"

"Of course you can," she gave a feisty nod and wink. It pleased her to deal with Mitch even at one remove. "And you're to make sure he does it."

"For you? He'd do anything," I told her.

But so would I.

Teaching

M Y FIRST DAY IN THE SCHOOL it became obvious some standoff stood between the two men. I saw it at break.

"What's this I hear? You're taking an Irish class?" a voice came at my back. I was at the table pouring a cup of tea. The big metal pot was dented and heavy, its handle hot. It must have taken many scaldings in the school. I put it down carefully so as not to twist my wrist and turned.

"That's right. I just had them. Isn't it a kick?" I tossed off the incongruity with a light laugh. His face told me no. He just kept looking at me. I sipped my tea. It tasted scorched.

"Well, it's only a hiccup. It won't last. They're switching the timetable. Do you need some tea?" I steered clear of trouble. The way he squared his blockish body in front of me I felt it coming.

"I'm grand," he put forth his cup with a clumsy jerk to show it was full. Tea sloshed onto the saucer. A biscuit leaning against the cup soaked it up. "Tell me how you got on?"

"The kids made it easy," I talked freely, ignoring the challenge in his voice. "The minute I walked in one of them said, 'You're not teaching *us*, are you Miss?' That was my cue. 'No,' I told him. '*You* are going to teach *me*.'"

He smiled more genially than I expected but was a mess to look at. His lips pulled wide, the lower one was fleshy, heavy, protruding. It could have held a pipe on both ends at the same time. Soggy biscuit sat on it now. There was only one tooth apparent, an upper-front incisor stood neither left nor right but dead centre.

"First Years, was it?" he asked and brushed his hand across his mouth not noticing that the crumbs stuck to the cuff of his tweed jacket.

"Right, First Years. What subject do you teach?"

"Geography," he said, his west Cork accent hit the 'jaw' and swallowed the rest. "And what Irish were they able to teach you?"

I sipped again. Another teacher sitting at a nearby window caught my eye. He sat so straight the support of the stiff-backed chair seemed superfluous. He sat still too, alert to our conversation, or so I sensed, even though he did not look our way. It was like when you walk cautiously through the woods, going softly and stepping lightly so as not to disturb what might be lurking. But then a twig snaps or there's a rustle. You stop, you listen and it's then you hear the quiet even sharper.

"They couldn't teach me much," I told the man facing me.

"Is that so?" He twisted his head to the side and looked with scrutiny.

"I mean I couldn't learn much," I hurried to make it clear the fault was with me. That smoothed his face.

"What was it you learned, so?" He pressed me for specifics.

"Well, I started by asking them to tell me about Diarmuid agus Gráinne or Queen Maebh, Children of Lír, Cú Chulainn—is that how you pronounce it?"

"Coo-chulinn," he gutturaled the second syllable like clearing catarrh.

"Okay," I didn't try it myself. "They moaned anyway at the mention of the myths and legends. They must be old hat to them. So I asked if there are any local stories and they told me about the tree on Sheehan's land.

"I thought they were joking but they were not. They really believe fairies live in and around the tree. They say they won't go into the field. They've been warned off. 'By bigger kids?' I asked. No, their parents tell them they better stay away or else. Can you believe that?" I asked him.

"And why wouldn't I?" He didn't tell me one way or another.

"Well I asked them for proof, like had anyone seen the fairies and they said no, you can't see them. The proof is the things that happen to people who go into the field. And boy did they have examples, one after another, on and on ... a man's cow died or a woman who never fell before tripped on nothing and broke her arm and there's a man whose pipe started disappearing, he could never find it where he left it. I could hardly stop them.

"But I said, 'That's all hearsay and maybe it's just coincidence. Have any of you ever put it to the test?' I looked at a spunky one who'd be most likely to challenge a piseog. Know what he said? 'Why don't you test it yourself, Miss?'"

"He's good enough for you. Must be young Coakley."

We chuckled.

"'No way. You guys win,' I told them and surrendered. I don't want to be in their bad books."

"Ah, it's easy enough to bring them along," he said and glanced ever so slightly over his shoulder towards the straight-backed chair. "So long as you don't take it too seriously."

The straight-backed teacher turned his head slightly and looked out of the window. He slit his eyes, maybe against the sun.

"I better get back to class," I said, glad my break was over just then. "See you again, I'm sure."

"Right so. I'm Donncha," the 'ch' sprayed.

I told him my name. We shook hands.

One day the next week Donncha came into break carrying a bunch of rolled up charts. He had them tucked under his low arm, the side he limped to. He didn't seem to realise how wide the scrolls made him. Instead of negotiating the narrow aisle between the tables, Donncha ambled ahead as usual. A scroll rammed into the back of a chair. It jerked Donncha's grip. The lot of them dropped, flopped and tumbled onto the floor. They rolled helter-skelter mainly towards Aodh, the man on the straight-backed chair. He sat unperturbed, one thin leg crossed over the other so precisely both of his feet touched the floor. The charts lay there in a trail in front of him.

Donncha went after them, bending and scooping them into his arms, clasping them to his chest. At Aodh's feet he crouched on one knee to pull in the final two. Aodh didn't move a muscle except to lift the cigarette he held poised between his thin, stained fingers. He drew deep but did not exhale until Donncha struggled up and carried his armfuls away.

"Here you go," I followed Donncha with a scroll that had bounced on end to me.

"These are after coming down from Dublin in today's post." Donncha settled them on a table at the window end of the room, the only table not filled with tins, bowls, weighing scales, ingredients, utensils and other paraphernalia for baking. We took our break in the Domestic Science room.

He lifted a scroll, spied down it as through a telescope, rejected it and tried another. This one he unfurled and secured flat with two saucers and a book. I slipped my saucer onto the fourth corner so he could free his hand.

"This will become a collector's item." He hunched over the map. It was of Europe. He inspected it, fingering over the lands as slowly as a farmer paces his fields after a storm.

"How come?" I asked, not noticing anything remarkable. But then my view was almost completely blocked by Donncha's rounded torso roving over the continent.

"Once this EEC is inaugurated 'twill all be English. Or French. They won't be bothered making maps of Europe that mark out the details in Irish," he told me.

"Oh?" I said, encouraging him to tell me more. But a voice came from behind us.

"Utter nonsense!," it said, not loud but the measured tone and clipped pronunciation penetrated the tea and talk. The room hushed. Donncha's back reared up slowly. I stepped aside.

"You think so, do you?" Donncha turned directly to Aodh who remained resolutely side-faced.

"The truly committed remain steadfast when their

language and culture come under threat," Aodh spoke like someone making a pronouncement.

"And the true European can see the reality of the times we are living in," Donncha's tone and words also sounded like he was reading a script.

Cups, spoons and saucers clicked gently. Colleagues stacked them cautiously so as not to crack the tight air and then walked soundlessly to the door, women on tiptoe, holding their hollow high heels up from the lino.

"We aren't in Europe yet," Aodh looked down and stubbed out his cigarette in the ashtray on his lap. Exhaling his final drag he enveloped himself in smoke.

"The treaty is as good as signed," Donncha put forth.

"Signed or no, it isn't every treaty rests easy with the people," Aodh stood up. From across the room the two men held a searing look. I left.

One Friday a notice was stuck to the break room door. Black ink on white paper, it could have looked stark except that it was handwritten in Celtic script. The thin strokes and thickening curves flowed delicately in a slight forward slant, light and very even. A gentle hand must have guided the nib. One line was larger than the other: 'Deireadh Seachtaine Gaelach.'

"Should I know what's on the notice?" I asked Donncha. He had beckoned me to look at one of his new charts. It was of wild flowers. He read out the names but I couldn't take in the Irish.

"Lovely," I said when at last he stopped. "What about the notice?"

"Himself put it up," Donncha tossed his head towards

Aodh, rolled up the chart and went to the table with the biscuit tin. Aodh looked over. I was left standing in the crossfire which was tedious. I wasn't on anyone's side. I went over to Aodh. He saw me coming and turned his head away.

"Excuse me." I kept my voice soft so he wouldn't come to life too fast. "Can you tell me what the notice says?" He turned his fine featured face towards me. His eyes were clear, watery and blue.

"There is to be an Irish weekend, a fortnight from tomorrow in the hotel," he said and looked away again. In black and white, in a language I didn't know, on a notice taped to the door the information was more inviting.

"What goes on?" I asked trying to be friendly, maybe draw him out. He turned to me again, slowly. It seemed like an effort of will.

"There's a seanchaí, a san-nós singer, ceol agus a céilí." I waited for him to tell me more, somehow break it down so I could understand. He didn't. He took a smoke.

"What's with Aodh?" I asked Brian that afternoon on our way to Cork. Brian was the woodwork teacher. He was building a house just off the Bandon Road a few miles outside Cork. The frame was up, roofed and all. Plaster work and floorboards were finished. Brian worked every weekend on things like window boards, skirting, door frames and light fixtures. He talked most enthusiastically about the stairway. It was to be freestanding, railings on both sides and he was shaping the thirty-two rail spokes himself from teak he'd come across by accident because someone knew someone who, etc. Brian was quiet unless talking about the house which he did in scrupulous detail. I was glad to introduce another topic.

"He's not the worst."

"Why doesn't he engage?"

"He keeps to himself."

This was getting nowhere.

"Is there some scuttle? If it's none of my business, that's okay. You don't have to tell me. It's just that I'd know how to approach him or even whether to approach. Is something the matter?"

"Nothing's the matter," Brian hugged a bend rounding it at fifty miles per hour. I tightened my grip on the armrest, dug my heels into the floor.

Brian was engaged, getting married in three months. He hadn't told me her name but let it slip she lived in Cork. After dropping me at UCC every Friday I suspected he went to her. That's why he drove like blazes over the sixty miles of twisting narrow road.

"Does it bother him to sit alone at break?" I persisted.

"Doesn't seem to."

"Is he avoiding someone?"

Brian shrugged.

"What I want to know," I quit hedging, "is did he and Donncha fall out over something?"

"Oh, that. It's ... " Brian started to speak but then saw his chance on the road. He hunched forward, gripped the wheel, jerked into the oncoming lane and started to overtake, uphill, a long truck. He'd crossed a solid line. I closed my eyes until I felt us swerve back to safety. Brian didn't resume the conversation. I had to.

"About Aodh and Donncha."

"It's Irish. They fell out over it. When Aodh retired he took over Donncha's classes."

"Retired? Isn't he teaching every day?"

"Only a few classes a week," Brian's prematurely bald temple began to redden. He lurched the car up to menace the slow driver in front of us.

"What did he used to do?"

"Principal."

"Where?"

"With us. Fourteen years."

"Doesn't Donncha like teaching Geography? He sure can talk about it."

"Anyone can teach Geography," Brian said.

"What do you mean? I couldn't," I said. I felt compelled to stand up for Donncha even though my goodwill towards him was wearing thin. He targeted me at every break.

"No, you took me up wrong. For the likes of Donncha and Aodh Irish is the main thing schools should teach and only the chosen are capable of teaching it."

"Ah, I see. So when Aodh took Donncha's Irish classes, Donncha felt demoted or sidelined."

"There's more to it than that."

"Oh?" I prodded when Brian didn't continue.

"It's the whole bloody language thing," his tone took an edge. "They drum it into you in school. But I never minded that. I actually liked Irish and I was good at it. It was after I left school."

Brian stopped speaking. I checked the road. He had overtaken the slow car with ease. There was nothing pressing in front of us. I moved the conversation ahead gently.

"Did something happen?"

"You don't come across Irish very often so you don't get a chance to speak it. But I heard of a group that met in a local pub and decided to go along. It took me a few weeks to work up the courage. My Irish was rusty. I'd been teaching a few years but hadn't spoken Irish conversationally since I left Uni. In I went. The place was singing with Irish. I bided my time, stayed standing at the bar.

"They knew I was new but not one of them made the slightest effort. No one came near me. I finished my first pint without speaking a word, English or Irish. Halfway down the second pint I got annoyed. I wasn't going to be shut out. I picked up my pint and went over to the crowd that looked easiest to get into. They were about my own age, laughing now and again, having a good time. The older ones sat in a tight circle. They frowned and nodded and murmured like they were plotting the Second Coming."

I laughed. Brian didn't.

"They made room for me and kept talking, one of them in particular. He had a great flow, very fast. I had to listen but managed to make out more than I expected. I was feeling fairly relaxed when of a sudden your man looked at me and asked a question.

"I repeated it over in my mind to make sure I had it straight and then I formed an answer, in my mind like, to be sure of it. The circle had gone quiet, all of them looking at me, waiting. Here goes, I thought and spoke the first words of Irish I'd said in more than five years—and didn't make a bad job of it, either. Or so I thought until your man, quick as a flash, corrected my grammar, two mistakes in as many sentences. After that I was dropped. They left me out of the conversation. No one took up the point I made or tried to bring me in again. Once the grammar's not right, the purists won't have you."

"What about this weekend thing Aodh has going? It seems open to everyone, the notice is all over town, anyway. I saw it in the post office, the chemist, the VG."

"That's only because Aodh sent some of the lads off out of class to put them up."

"Will you be going?"

"Wouldn't go near the place." Brian put on the indicator, turned right off the Western Road and made a U-turn aiming back out again at the old prison gates, down near La Retraite at UCC.

"Even if there are lots of people there?" I thought it was a school-spirited thing to support a colleague's effort and imagined most of the teachers and half the town turning up.

"Lots of people?" Brian repeated my words in a snoot. He put the gear into neutral, let the engine idle and thought a minute. "There'll be Aodh's clique and Donncha's crowd and a few other factions from around the place. If the thing gets going at all, that is."

He shifted gear to reverse and revved the engine. The fiancée must have been waiting.

"Thanks for the lift," I said, reached for my rucksack on the back seat and pulled it to the front carefully so as not to hit the gearstick. The sack was heavy. I had copies to correct.

"See you Monday morning," he said as I got out.

"Slánleat," I chanced a bit of Irish just before closing the car door.

"Any more of that and you'll be thumbing next Friday," he called out his window and laughed. Good. He'd be in a good mood for herself.

"The reins slip through the horse dealer's hands in the rain,"

I called out the sentence to the First Years. I was dictating sentences for them to diagram that night. It was Wednesday afternoon, market day in the town square. Our classroom on the second storey overlooked the stalls, vans and carts set up under blankets of canvas. A horse reluctant to come out of its box was giving its owner a hard time.

"You can't trick us, Miss," young Sheehan said. "Anyone knows the difference between rain and reins."

"Next line then—and this is not dictation. It's a question. What figure of speech are rein and rain?"

"Ah, Miss. You said dictation," Sheehan complained.

"Not fair," another boy mumbled, put down his biro and folded his arms in protest.

Heads turned and scowled at the two boys, attention seekers.

"Oh, come on. Just think. We worked on figures of speech all last week." I turned the corner of one row and paced up the other.

"Give us a clue, Miss," a girl coaxed.

"Look what's coming!" a boy on the window row pointed outside.

We all looked. A procession of cars flashed onto the square.

"Who's he?" I asked when a man stepped out of the back seat of the biggest car, the door and an umbrella held open for him.

"Malachy Merc."

"He's the TD."

"Shaking hands for the by-election."

The class filled me in.

"Okay. We've seen him. Sentence number two: Malachy canvassed under the sheets of canvas."

Some chuckled. More rolled their eyes. Most just wrote.

I was watching the politician glad-hand his way through stalls hung with plastic rain gear, woolly jumpers, copper pots and trinkets, vegetables and so on when I saw a procession coming against him. It was Donncha leading his class of about fifteen students. A couple of them carried trowels. Malachy Merc proffered a hand. But Donncha was head-bent in his own direction. Malachy withdrew the hand and stepped aside. I couldn't tell whether Donncha had seen it or not.

"They're on the tear, Miss," a voice cut across my staring.

"Okay. No more distractions," I walked over to the far wall to take their attention away from the windows and to cut out my own view.

"They've gone for the fossils, Miss," said one.

"The Neanderthal man," said another.

"Sentence number three—unless you want to write these after school?" I stopped their laughing.

"Where'd you take your class yesterday?" I asked Donncha at break next morning.

"Digging," he said.

"For what?"

"You'll see soon enough," he smiled so I'd ask more.

"When?"

"The weekend."

"This one?"

"The Derieadh Seachtaine Gaelach."

I did not catch it right away.

"Oh, yeah," it clicked.

"I'll be speaking," Donncha lifted his chin.

"For Aodh?" I tried to keep surprise out of my voice.

"For the people," he said in a way that sounded patriotic. He drank back his tea and left. Aodh's eyes flickered. He watched Donncha go. Maybe he sat tighter too which did not bode well for the weekend next after this, though there was no talk about it. Nothing had been mentioned, said or announced since the signs went up three weeks ago. I expected Aodh to break out of isolation and drum up some interest. I kept an eye out in case a list of speakers would be posted so I could tell Mitch. Since nothing had appeared, I went across the square to the hotel after school on Thursday to check out any information.

"'Lo, Miss," two girls said in unison. They hooked arms at the elbow and stepped aside as one to let me step up the kerb.

"Hi," I put on a bright smile and held the 'i' a long time to be as friendly as possible. This pair were in fifth year. I had seen students step out of their way in the corridors and watched them waylay younger kids at the gate before and after school. I didn't teach them, thank goodness. With the cut of an eye they could get a class to stonewall you.

"Thank you," I stepped deftly past them. Walking up the hotel steps I glanced back. Their smirking eyes watched me.

The hotel was old and dark. No one was at the front desk so I looked into the lounge. No one there but a man standing at the bar, the bartender getting drinks and a young woman sitting alone on the cushion-backed long seat in the corner of the room. Dark hair, dark clothes, if it wasn't for the light coming in the window near her I would not have seen her there at all.

I heard voices in the foyer and turned to see two women—one the housekeeper, for she wore a shapeless dress with blue apron, Scholl sandals and carried a stack of clean towels, the other the receptionist in smart skirt and high heels. They were coming down the stairs. The bottom one moaned under their weight.

"May I help you?" the receptionist focused her attention on me right away.

"I'm just looking for information about the Irish weekend."

She looked puzzled.

"It's being held here, the weekend after this," I reminded her though I couldn't imagine the hotel being that busy she would forget a big booking.

She went around the desk, bent her head to a large black book and turned over a few pages. "Here 'tis. The Deireadh Seachtaine Gaelach?" she asked.

"That's it." The words were immediately familiar by now. "Have you got a schedule? Of what's going on?"

"No. Just the booking. It was made a good few weeks ago and we've heard nothing about it since. Wouldn't they be able to tell you over at the school? Isn't it they're organising it?"

"Oh, right. Good idea," I said knowing I looked foolish. But I couldn't tell her I'd come across the square to circumvent Aodh. As I turned from the desk the door to the lounge closed on someone who had slipped neatly through it. He was small built and had a shock of white hair and yes, when I passed and looked in through the glass panel it was he, Aodh, walking niftily through the low, empty tables. I noticed too that the young woman was still sitting alone, the man who'd been at the bar earlier had not joined her. He sat on a high stool, his elbows leaning on a newspaper spread open on the counter.

"Looks to me as if it's going to be a bit of a rí-rá," I said.

Mitch and I were talking about the weekend while we ate. He wanted to be there early enough on Sunday to take in the afternoon session. I did not want to attend. It would cut short our weekend.

"Aodh has quite a reputation," he told me and passed the butter after taking a chunk for his potatoes.

"For what?"

Mitch picked up my scepticism and snapped his brown eyes. He could be prickly about things Gaeilge.

"He's a native speaker and was quite a teacher in his day, not just in the VEC. He taught on summer courses for teachers in the Gaeltacht."

"Did he ever get married?" I was hoping maybe he'd once softened to a summer romance. I sprinkled salt on my carrots and turnip, two vegetables I cooked hoping to acquire a taste.

"How would I know?" Mitch treated the question like it was off the subject whereas getting a handle on Aodh was the only thing that interested me in the weekend. "It would be good to support him," he said.

We left Cork early on the Sunday to be in time for the closing session. When we drove into town just after noon there was no space to park in the square. We found a place up a steep, narrow side street and left the car half on, half off the sidewalk, so close to the terraced house I could have seen right into its small, recessed front window but for the net curtain and bright geranium on the inside ledge. Walking down the empty pavement our footsteps followed us in echo. Nothing else stirred.

All the action was in the hotel. The lounge was so packed people stood in the foyer, drinks in hand. A fug of smoke and cacophony of voices escaped out of the lounge when Mitch put his head through the door looking for the Irish crowd. A red-faced, round man came out of the dining-room. A red-faced, round woman followed as did the heavy aroma of cooked meat, vegetables, gravy and conversation. No signs, no-one at reception, we walked ahead, down a short corridor, around a corner, through a door and from there the muffled sound of a tin whistle led us to the function room where we belonged. It was as barren as the upstairs had been bulging. No more than forty people were scattered on chairs set up for a hundred. I was glad we could fill two seats.

The two arm-linked girls sat on the front row, their eyes rapt in bright attention at a young man playing the tin whistle. One girl noticed us and nudged the other. They gave Mitch a keen once-over. A burst of clapping followed the whistler when he finished and walked out of the hollow hall. Mitch and I went to seats near the back row.

Donncha was next. He walked across the front of the room in long strides that made his limp more noticeable. He went to a bare dining table shoved against the wall and dragged it out centre. The two girls were quick to help. Heavy stones on the table did not budge as it stuttered across the carpet tiles. Donncha asked one of the girls to stay up front, standing alongside the table. She tugged the waist of her miniskirt and smoothed it down along her hips as if trying to put some length in it.

Donncha began. He spoke forth in Irish. His large arms and hands made gestures big enough for a large, outdoor arena pointing at intervals to one or other of the stones. As he did, the girl would lift it up high so we could all see as

Donncha commented on its features. These, I gathered when he poked his two fingers into indentations at the top of a roundish stone and then pointed to his eyes, were his fossils. He went on for such a long time his voice became a drone in my ear. I watched other people. They were catching eyes and laughing softly at Donncha's serious intent.

When his assistant realised no-one was paying close attention she started to look bored and might have descended into sullen except Tin Whistle came back. He had a pint, its foamy head already gulped well down the glass. He took a seat up front. The girl concentrated her attractions on him. The space between them became magnetic. Watching her, Tin Whistle wiped pint off his lips with the back of his hand while she wrapped her fleshy fingers ever more tautly around each fossil putting so much pressure on one it popped out of her hands right onto the floor.

"Ow-ooch!" The girl hopped and bent and held a foot. Her mate, the girl that is, went quickly to her side and put an arm around her before Tin Whistle might. Donncha chased the rolling stone. A listener scuttled under his chair to help retrieve it. Aodh appeared then and stood in front of us to bring a bit of hush. The fallen rock had caused an outburst of laughing. The wounded girl limped to a seat, not her own but one next to Tin Whistle.

Aodh started speaking. He stood still, one hand in his jacket pocket the other at his chest, two fingers slipped between the buttons of his waistcoat. Small framed, he cut a dapper figure. His voice did not bounce around the room like Donncha's but was soft. The room had to be quiet to hear him and everyone was listening except Donncha. He was at the table behind Aodh positioning the stones as precisely as billiard balls shaped by a frame. He belaboured his business and became a distraction like the unwitting passer-by behind a TV newsman. A tension started. Aodh's eyes shifted left towards Donncha. Donncha remained impervious. The room began to grow tight but then, as if from nowhere, she appeared, entirely unnoticed until now.

She walked right up to Donncha, slipped close beside him and placed her hand so gently on his worn, tweed sleeve it was a wonder he felt it. But he did and stopped instantly. He turned his head and met her face to face. She whispered lightly. Donncha's eyes moved slowly along her face, over its pure skin and refined cast of features. Neither fossil nor fairy could work such a phantom magic upon him. He might have walked on air. Instead he hunched down and walked back to his seat carefully rolling each foot from heel to toe. The right shoe squeaked.

The distraction gone, Aodh resumed speaking, his watery blue eyes dancing, glancing repeatedly towards the young woman sitting now at the far end of the front row. Watching her profile to see whether she responded to Aodh's attention, her crinkly jet-black hair started to seem familiar. I pushed my memory and there she was, right here in the hotel, not downstairs but up in the lounge last week when I came to enquire about the weekend. She had been sitting alone until, of course—Aodh slipped through the door and joined her.

Clapping cut across my discovery. Aodh had extended his hand towards Donncha who stood to robust applause. Tin Whistle put his pint on the floor between his heavy boots and cupped his two hands around his mouth. He whistled and the whistling rang the air. The girl friends pealed with laughter. They clapped to outdo each other with gusto.

Someone whooped. I clapped even though I had not understood one word the whole afternoon. I was applauding the message in Aodh's hand, out-turned towards Donncha. Mitch went up to Aodh as soon as Aodh had finished his closing remarks. The young woman joined them and the three talked a long time, smiling and laughing often.

"So this is what you and your class were up to," I said. Donncha was wrapping the fossils one by one in newspaper and packing them into a 'Batchelors Beans' grocery box.

"Didn't we go on a good day?"

"It was an awful day, pouring rain," I recalled all the stalls covered with tarps.

"And isn't that the luck of it? The ground was soft and the stream flowing. There was very little digging in it for the lads and no damage to the fossils. The running water cleaned away the soil without a bother. We could see what we had right away."

"How do you know if a stone's a fossil and not just a rock?" I asked Donncha what I would have asked earlier if his talk hadn't been cut short and if I could speak Irish.

"There's plenty by the stream where the soil's silty," he told me.

"But they aren't all fossils," I pointed out.

"Of course they're not."

"So how can you tell the difference?"

"You look at them."

"Yes ... " I drawled, coaxing him.

"And you see the shape and the line, the curve of it." Donncha picked up one of the two fossils still not wrapped and pointed out its features, features apparent to him anyway. He saw something in an imprint. Cross my heart and stretch my eye, I could not see it.

"Right," I left it at that and glanced over towards Mitch. He was still talking. Like Brian, I knew better than to intrude on the Irish. Very carefully I picked up the last stone, re-nestled it into the crumpled hold of a double sheet of newspaper and laid it to rest in the box.

"Give us a hand to the car," Donncha held out his keys. I took them and watched his broad shoulders and back pull the heavy box off the table. I followed at a distance ready to skedaddle if the box fell and rocks rolled. Donncha, however, did not falter. Having found a task worthy of them, his limbs and feet moved with assurance.

His big old car was parked just around the corner. One side sagged into the kerb. I wrenched open the trunk.

"Clear a space, can't you?" Donncha was short of breath so I took a deep one and burrowed into the clutter, unearthing and shifting the paraphernalia: a mud covered trowel and wellington boots, rope, pliers, a closed biscuit tin that clattered with who knew what. I lifted and tugged a jumper. It was snagged on the rusty tine of a pitchfork.

"Leave it. 'Twill cushion the box," Donncha cut short my tug of war and wedged his box into the hole I had dug. He whammed the trunk lid and whopped it shut which startled a dog napping against a door and set off a yelp, not from the dog but from back around the corner. There came the girls with Tin Whistle and now another fella too. They passed us in twosomes, arms interlocked around waists.

"'Lo, Sir."

"'Lo, Miss."

Donncha and I stepped wide to let them pass.

"Hi," I watched them go. Tin Whistle's girl had her fingers in the back pocket of his cords.

Aodh, Mitch and the woman came out of the hotel door. Mitch and I declined the offer of a drink. Friends in the next town expected us for tea. The woman smiled and spoke to Donncha.

"Go raibh maith agat," he said, his smile a boyish grin.

She slipped her hand through Aodh's arm. Donncha went with them back into the hotel.

"Aodh knows her from a summer course," Mitch told me. That's all he knew, except that she was a teacher and where she taught.

"She could be good for him," I supposed out loud but drew no answer. Mitch has no curiosity where it matters.

Next day at break Aodh took up his place apart and Donncha cornered me. The weekend seemed to have changed nothing.

"Have you a free class during the week?" he asked.

"Two in a row Thursday afternoon. Why?"

"Thursday," he thought. "'Twould do."

"What for?"

"I'll be taking the Second Years one of the days. It might as well be the Thursday. I need new fossils for Aodh and herself. They've asked me to speak on the summer course. You can come along with the class Thursday after next," he offered.

"I'd love to. But I can't. This is my last week. Where do you go?"

"Out the road to Sheehan's field," he told me.

"Sheehan's field? As in fairy tree Sheehan?"

"The same," his heavy fingers worked like they were numb trying to open a packet of cream crackers.

"Doesn't it scare you?" I took the packet, opened it and held the opened end out to him.

"Don't be daft," he took and bit a cracker hard. Crumbs sprayed down and landed on his jumpered tummy.

"What about the kids? They told me they're afraid."

"I tell them the fairies are there minding the fossils until we dig them out." More crumbs flew through the air as he spoke.

"Now who's daft? They don't fall for that," I said.

"I also remind them field trips take the place of homework," he winked and tipped his face to the side. "'Tis a pity you can't come to see for yourself."

Maybe so. But fairies, fossils, fields off limits—I didn't want to dig into all that. Wasn't there enough to uncover above ground?

Baby

Weight loss.
Low grade nausea.
Some overall swelling.
Places tender to the slightest touch ...

YOU'D THINK A WOMAN WOULD KNOW! But a doctor had to tell me. Oh, and there was the missed period but that had happened before, the time I stayed too long on a rigid diet. Being told I was pregnant made the weeks of non-specific symptoms add up to something concrete and that's about as far as I could think. My imagination would not stretch to the reality that in thirty-two weeks Mitch and I would have a baby. Cousin Cáit, however, put me in the picture when we went to the house to tell her and John. Cáit and I were in the kitchen.

"In March?" she turned off the tap and stopped peeling the potatoes. Looking straight ahead out of the window over the sink she frowned against the sunlight and reckoned. "By then ye'll be married what? Two and a half years, is it?"

"I guess." Cáit calculates better than me.

"That's it! Two and a half years." She was sure. Turning to me she aimed the blade of a paring knife at me. "You should consider yourself lucky. I just barely got the year," she said and took a slick peeled potato out of the colander, held it down on the draining board and cut it, thwack, in two.

"I'm not so surprised," Mrs. O'Neill gave my face a good looking over when I told her and then she took up her knitting again. I waited. She would have more to say. The needles jabbed in and out in a steady clicking rhythm that lulled me into staring. My eyes rested on the knitting and then started stepping up the moss stitches, swerving down the cable lanes and around the blackberries. Mrs. O'Neill put a stop to my roving eye when she dropped her hands to her lap. The sweater front crumpled under them.

"That explains your face," she said. I looked at her. A scolding was about to begin but I didn't mind. It was a comfort just now to be treated like a child. Mrs. O'Neill's sea-blue eyes sparkled with intent. "You're drawn looking. The bloom's gone off you. But it's no wonder the way you only nibble at the cakes or scones when you call. And it was you used to carry them back into the kitchen to prevent yourself finishing the lot. You'll have to stop that slimming nonsense and get proper meals inside you."

But inside me had taken over. I was queasy all the time. The nausea drove me to taking walks miles longer than usual going no place in particular all around Cork city. When I got tired of running in circles I figured out some destinations. From our house I went way out to the Curraheen Road or further to the back road that went to Macroom. Or I bused to town and headed out to Glanmire along the dual carriageway one day, the Cobh Road another. Weekends Mitch and I drove out to walk along the quiet, hedged-in roads around Youghal, Mallow, Kinsale and Fermoy. Eventually inside me settled down.

I joined a natural childbirth class. There were nine of us. Our instructor was Mrs. Prunty, once a full-time nurse. Every Wednesday morning Mrs. Prunty set out mats around the perimeter of a large bright room on the first floor of the hospital. We lay down on our backs and followed her instructions through a series of breathing, bending and twisting exercises so gentle they almost soothed me to sleep, which might have been the aim.

"Giving birth is a normal, natural thing. It does not require the intervention of drugs," Mrs. Prunty repeated her soothsayer's mantra throughout every class. Her voice floated out from a large chest and through a bright smile. You could almost believe her.

One Wednesday she proved her point.

"I've a treat for you today," she announced, her smile extra bright. I looked beside her chair at the over-filled tote bag she carried. It bulged bigger than usual. Cravings had replaced the nausea. I hoped she'd brought us natural juices and granola bars, the kind of snack she recommended.

"We'll do our exercises first although I may have to cut them a bit short to allow for time," a frown creased her third eye. Mrs. Prunty didn't like compromising valuable exercise time.

Midway through the session there was a gentle knock at

the door. Mrs. Prunty arched back her shoulders and cocked an ear. The knock came again but with no more force.

"Just keep breathing," she waved her hands like bellows over us as she stepped quickly to the door. She opened it just wide enough to slip outside, carefully keeping it ajar in case one of us should suddenly need her. She spoke to someone in the hall in a whisper. She stood half in, half out of the room, her presence necessary to both sides of the door.

"In your own time," we knew this meant right away, "you may return to sitting," she told us and watched us roll from our backs to our sides and get up onto all fours as she had instructed us. From there we came to standing. Once we were all seated on the chairs set one apiece at the heads of our mats, Mrs. Prunty disappeared out the door for a few brief moments. When she came back in she was beaming. She stretched her arm out fully like a vaudevillian compère and beckoned someone to come forth.

A young woman walked in. She cradled a small bundle in her folded arms. Mrs. Prunty closed the door and dashed to the tote bag. She pulled out a cushion, not snacks, and plumped it, squared it onto a chair and stood the chair out centre where all of us could see. She spun round and took the baby so mother could sit.

"Baby James is just two days old," Mrs. Prunty held him up facing our direction then handed him into his mother's upstretched arms. "And mother's delivery was completely normal and natural," she smiled upon James' mother and clapped. We joined in. Mother kept her eyes fixed on the face swaddled in the crook of her arm.

Mrs. Prunty invited questions. I recoiled. Giving birth might well be normal and natural but it is also private.

What question could be asked that wouldn't be indelicate? An intrusion? But Mrs. Prunty waited, her eyebrows held up, inviting, coaxing. When a few questions came Mrs. Prunty became an interpreter. She restated each one and then embellished the mother's one-word or short phrase answers, for mother, whose name we never got, spoke in a very soft voice and lifted her eyes only briefly when she spoke. I heard the details but they weren't any of my business so I didn't allow them into my mind.

The delivery date for our baby came and went. The gynaecologist did not seem perturbed so neither were we until the second Sunday baby was overdue. Cáit caught sight of us in church and drew herself on me after Mass. She rained down a check list of questions that trailed back through the forty weeks, only stopping just short of conception. No doctor ever penetrated a patient's history as fast. My answers did not please her. Cáit is keen for trouble but the pregnancy had progressed without incident. And besides, the graver she got the more determined I was to be blithe.

"I'm telling you," she brought me to book with a portentous look. "You're to phone that doctor of yours and you're to tell him you want something done. Tomorrow. You tell him you'll not wait, not one day longer. Do you hear me?"

"Yes," I said but only to appease her and stop the sidelong looks from passers-by. She withdrew her index finger from my face.

Tuesday afternoon I walked up Patrick's Hill to my scheduled appointment. I was ambivalent about the birth. The longer baby waited, the longer nature could take care without diapers, babygrows, cream, oil, cotton wool, bottles, formula, steriliser, cot, blankets, pram. But nature has a mind of its own and so does the doctor.

"If nothing happens during the night, we'll get things going tomorrow morning," the doctor was writing on a pad as he spoke. The light coming in the window behind his desk shone right through his thinning hair, exposing his pale scalp. "When you give this note to Sister she'll give you a bed tonight." I heard him but chose to listen to his fountain pen. It scratched out the final few words of the note and when he tore the page from the gummy binding it made a hacking sound like a throat clearing. Doctor folded the note in two, pressed it into an envelope, licked it and sealed our fate. "You'll be induced in the morning."

"Okay. Thank you," I stood up to go. I didn't know what 'induced' meant and even though he smiled and was pleasant, the doctor never made eye contact long enough to take questions. So I didn't ask any and that was that.

And this is it, I realised when I got outside and stood looking down Bridge Street and onto Patrick's, my last afternoon. Before I knew what I was doing I was inside a pastry shop sitting at a table. The waitress set a three-tiered cake stand in front of me. In under five minutes I had ravished three pastries, didn't matter which. For nine months my snacks had been carrot sticks, apples and pears to make sure the baby was nourished, my system in order and my weight within the limit. Craving had waited a long time to be satisfied. To prolong the pleasure I bought a Battenberg and apple tart on the way out to have for dessert that evening. It was late, time to walk to UCC and meet Mitch.

"We can stop by the hospital now," he suggested when I told him what the doctor said.

"No. It's okay. We'll go after the meal."

"We'll be passing right by. Then they'll know to expect you later," he pointed out.

"But I'm not ready."

"Ready for what? We're only telling them you'll be coming."

"I don't want to. Not before I have to."

"Don't be silly," he put on the clicker and drove in through the hospital gates.

The girl at reception took the doctor's note and asked us to take a seat and wait for Sister. When she came, Sister held the note, opened. We stood up.

"Come. I'll show you to your room," she said after we exchanged names.

"Now? I can't," I stepped back from her. It was too sudden. I wanted time alone with Mitch, a last meal in the ordinary luxury of our twosome. Sister raised an eyebrow.

"Mitch hasn't had dinner," I told her.

She turned to Mitch. She looked him up. She looked him down.

"Can he not look after himself?" she reached her hand as if to take my arm.

"I haven't packed my bag," I sidestepped closer to Mitch.

"Could you not do that for her?" Sister asked Mitch.

"I'd really rather do it myself," I said. This was not her territory.

"Have it your way," Sister conceded but not graciously. She turned and left us.

My roommate was already in bed for the night when I got

back to the hospital. She was there for her third baby to be induced the next day too. I read late to distract myself and slept well. Without breakfast the next morning my system felt in gear, ready for something else to satisfy it. At ten o'clock a nurse came and took me up in the elevator. In a room near the delivery ward I got into bed and was hooked up to a drip. All day I lay there. Four or five times a nurse came.

"Anything doing?" she'd ask and squint up at the drip bag for an answer.

"I don't think so," I'd say. I didn't know. I had no idea what to expect.

"You're grand then so," she'd check that the butterfly wing was still firmly in place on the back of my hand.

The morning dragged. Midday there was some activity. Two cleaning ladies came. They talked at a normal, outside volume, their voices amplified by the quiet in the room. One was telling the other about an encounter in Roches Stores. She'd had to put a shop girl in her place. They wheeled me out to the corridor so they could make a clean sweep of the floor. The one carrying the drip stand walked backwards. She misguided the metal rail headboard and we bumped the door jamb.

"Sorry pet," they both said, in unison, the first break in their conversation with each other.

"That's alright. I don't mind," I told them. It might get things moving. When they wheeled me back in they put me next to the windows that overlooked the back of the hospital. All I could see was the grey March sky bearing down low on the wet bare branches of the trees.

Late afternoon another bed was wheeled in. I paid no attention. The young woman in it seemed sound asleep. But after a little while from the corner of my eye I was aware of movement. I turned to look. Without a sound, as if her body was moving of its own accord, the woman's head and shoulders rose up off the pillows. Her face was without expression until her arms started to move. They pedalled the air, as if clawing to reach something and her face tormented itself through a series of contortions. She seemed locked in a tortured trance.

I was spellbound, maybe even horrified. I braced myself. Some primal scream was sure to come from her chalk-rimmed lips and exorcise her pain. But it didn't. Much more eerie, the woman subsided, lay back, soothed by some inner devil who kept her in thrall. The third time she rose I heard the Angelus. It tolled clearly from a not too distant church. Six o'clock. Mitch would be finishing his lecture just now. At the thought of him tears came and flowed down my face. And just then a Sister appeared at my bedside. She was a stout woman, wore her habit for action, the outer skirt pinned behind like a bustle, the veil was cut short to chin length to stay out of the way and her sleeves pushed above her elbows displaying forearms strong as a man's.

"Is something wrong?" she asked, looking at my wet face.

"No, Sister," I wiped it with my hands. "The tears just came. I'm really not crying."

"Let's take a look." She whipped back the sheet. I bared my tummy. She splayed the fingers of one hand on top of my tight belly and oscillated baby with vigour. She frowned, looked down, thought a minute.

"Will I give you something to help you along?" she asked, her hand resting on baby as naturally as a butcher touches a side of beef while he asks what size you want cut. I took 'help' to mean help the drip along, kick in some action.

"Yes," I sighed. This eight hour day felt longer than the nine months and two and a half weeks.

"Turn over to your side," Sister nudged my tummy in the direction of the wall. My body followed. A needle went into my hip. Her strong fingers kneaded the spot and the sheet came over me with a breeze. Sister was gone and so was I. I didn't wake until the next morning. I was being wheeled along a corridor. I opened my eyes. The rumbling and vibrating wheels stopped. A voice came through.

"You have a beautiful baby girl," someone said.

A nurse was smiling over me. She held a baby for me to see and yes, that baby was beautiful. She was wrapped in a white blanket. Her face had skin so new I raised my hands to touch and hold her but was asleep again before I could reach her. Next time I woke up I was in a bed back in my room. Mrs. Prunty was sitting down low at my feet.

"Not to worry. These things happen," she started consoling me when I opened my eyes.

"What's wrong? Is something wrong with our baby?" My mind was fully alert.

"No," she smiled. But I didn't trust her. She was a double-crosser. No, she hadn't actually administered the knockout shot but she had spent four months convincing me the whole thing would be normal and natural.

"You can tell me," I said in a voice with more force than I expected. I pressed my fists into the mattress and stiff-armed myself up the pillows to a sitting position. "Has something gone wrong?"

"No. Not at all. I've just come from the nursery and your

baby is sound asleep. She is perfect," her voice was soft, much softer than in class and she fixed her blue eyes on mine. They sparkled when she said 'perfect'. "How are you?" Her tone was confidential.

"Groggy," I said.

"You did a grand job they tell me," she patted my feet. So why did neither of us want to mention the final hours leading up to the birth and the birth itself? "But I must be off. It's Wednesday," her voice perked up. "Will I tell the class your good news?"

"Please do." For an instant I was grateful to the pethidine. It had spared me being brought forth for show and tell. "And thank you."

"Not at all," she stood and pulled her red cardigan, one side over each bosom.

Baby was an angel. She ate and slept as if born for discipline. To acquire some to suit her and whatever regime she would impose when we went home, I used the endless spare time in the hospital like a recruit in boot camp. I exercised. In bed, lying or sitting, I clenched inner, saggy muscles to reinvigorate elasticity. I walked miles of corridor on all floors and took the stairs not the elevator. My turn in the bath gave me the privacy to do sit ups and leg lifts. I became almost as fit as our drill sergeant.

Sister was in charge in the rooms on our end of the corridor and, if asked, could put herself in charge of God. She was about five feet tall and short-stepped bullet-like in and out of the rooms. She came to ours often. My roommate was having difficulty breastfeeding. Four or five times a day Sister arrived, snatched the curtain between our beds and drew it round its rim so fast it billowed from the gale force of her gait. She was not at all pleased when even on the third day after a long, failed session with a breast pump Joan would not have sense.

"But you gave your first two babies the bottle," I heard Sister argue.

"That's why. I'm determined to do it right this time," Joan told her.

"Then will you stop eating all those grapes," Sister wanted something to be Joan's fault. The natural childbirth classes were well established just two floors below. La Leche fliers were pinned to the notice board outside the nurses' station. Nature was threatening the efficient running of her corridor and Sister had to take it out on someone.

"The grapes are drying you up," she told Joan and clattered the breast pump, a metal contraption, back into its box. The curtain whipped open, its metal hooks clicked as fast as train wheels clacking over tracks at sixty miles per hour. "When will you have some sense and give your hungry child a bottle, like this young one here?" Sister stood between us, her hand held out towards me, the good patient on her right. I stared straight ahead and was certain Joan did too. We didn't dare catch each other's eye.

When it came to Sister I kept my head down until the afternoon I woke from a nap to find the morning's fresh draw sheet needed changing. No way would I call a nurse. I was able to change it myself if I could find a sheet in the linen cupboard. The corridor was in a lull like it always was after lunch before visitors started to come. I looked up and down. No nurse was about but I saw Sister just going into the staff-cum-store room. I approached the open door. She was sitting up straight up tight on a hard chair. Her elbows were pressed onto a table, her forearms raised holding her chin in her hands. She stared ahead at a blank wall. I swallowed and tapped lightly on the door held back with a chair. Sister did not move.

"Excuse me," I said, wincing at my voice. Though I kept it low, it seemed to resound. Sister did not turn or look at me but her head twitched like a dog when it catches a scent. "I'm sorry to bother you but my draw sheet needs changing and I can do it myself if you'll tell me where I can find a clean one," I said it all in one breath. "Please?" I added.

Sister did not budge. For a long five seconds the air held a tight silence. Suddenly came a sound like the crack of a whip. The open palms of her two hands lay flat on the table. She'd slapped it in temper. "Next thing you know they'll be saying they must change their own sheets," she railed against the wall she still stared at.

Then in a flash she was past me, a clean, folded sheet under her elbow. She had conjured it from nowhere. I followed to help but could not break in on her briskness. As deftly as a magician pulls the cloth from under a set table, Sister had the bed in order and was out the door before I could work up the courage to thank her.

By my fourth day in hospital I had counted the stairs and measured the paces up and down all corridors so often I would have begun a Biblical numbering of the hairs on baby's head except she had none. I was restless beyond reason to know when I could go home. So desperate to know when baby and I could leave, I decided to ask Sister. I planned my attack, for that's how she viewed questions, I was sure. Having felt the draught left in the wake of her speedy arrivals and exits from our room I knew I would have to spring it suddenly.

When she looked in that evening she went to Joan's bedside and complimented her for having replaced the bunch of grapes with a bottle of Mi Wadi orange drink. She merely glanced at me, I never needed anything unusual, and then started to go out of the room. Here was my only chance.

"Sister," I said. "Do you know when I'll be discharged?" I asked fast and used the hospital term to sound mature, capable of looking after baby at home alone.

Sister stopped dead in her tracks. She stood at the end of my bed, still looking straight out the door. Then, turning her head only, she clamped her eyes on my face and examined it. Under such scrutiny a hardened criminal would squirm. But I was a mother now and had to learn to stand my ground for baby and me. I smiled to show how healthy I was and to remind her that, bar the draw sheet incident, I had behaved impeccably. If for no other reason I deserved to be let out on good behaviour.

"Discharged?" Sister's entire face was askance. "Is there any doctor in this hospital or any other hospital would allow a washy looking one like you go home after only four days?" With that, before I could close my amazed mouth, she was out the door. And so was I next day to embark upon motherhood, however normal and natural it would be.

The Funeral

JACK WAS IN THE CHURCH FOR the night. Tom, his only brother, lived in England. He had sold the family farm sixteen years ago so after Jack's removal there was no particular place to gather. Some people went on home, some to the two village pubs, some to Jack's cousins' houses. Mitch and I went to Vera.

"We should be in Malachy's," Vera stood up red-faced from bending into the sideboard. She held the bottle of Jameson against her tummy and twisted the cap with such angry vigour it spun off the bottle and dropped to the floor.

"He's having everyone tomorrow, isn't he?" Mitch sat forward out of the fireside chair. The worn-out webbing crunched and moaned. He picked up the cap and set it on the dull silver tray next to a decanter that held the remains of a dark liquid made darker by the layer of dust covering the decanter's shoulders.

"And so what about it?" Vera dismissed Malachy's generosity opening the doors of his period house for the full funeral dinner next day. "Jack, God be good to him, should be stopping the night in Malachy's. Doesn't he deserve a proper wake after all those years working in the Wild West?"

"That's tons! That's tons!" Mitch raised his hand to stop the flow of whiskey. Vera had lost the run of her pouring. The glass was full, no room for the dilution Mitch preferred. But then Vera always poured it straight.

"Why should Jack be left in a cold chapel when there's a grand house not a mile out the road for him to come home to?" Vera poured a glass of Jameson for herself, sherry for me and sat rigid on the edge of a hassock covered in leather worn to wrinkles. Still its horsehair stuffing held firm. Vera's light frame made no indentation.

"Everyone has his own way of doing things," Mitch tried to mollify.

"And what is Malachy's way? Only to push aside anyone stands in it," Vera snapped. She sipped her drink and held it behind tight lips. She did not swallow. Her eyes stared out of the small window looking onto the village main street. We were in a tiny room, once a run-through between the house and the shop. The shop was sold years ago when Malachy, the ambitious eldest son, moved to the town ten miles away and set himself up in auctioneering. Vera lived alone, spent most of her time in this makeshift little room while upstairs the large parlour was left languishing in its past.

Which is where Vera's thoughts must be now, following her remark about Malachy pushing people aside. In a calculated step on his way to buying his period residence on twenty acres, Malachy had pulled off a clever land deal. At the time Vera was stepping out with a young man whose family's dwindling fortune needed propping up. Malachy had bought some land from them and sold it on within the year at a sizeable profit. The families fell out. Vera's courtship ended. She never set her heart on any other man.

"The church will be packed tomorrow, do you think?" Mitch drew Vera's mind back into the present.

Vera swallowed and closed her eyes to feel the drink go down.

"Jack was a good man, none better. But there was something lacking. Common sense," she tapped her temple. "Anyone who inherits half the proceeds from a thriving farm should take advice, invest the money. But not Jack. They say he squandered his share on the Red Indians. Wouldn't you think a wealthy place like America would look after its own instead of making a social welfare officer out of a priest from Ireland?"

"How do you know Jack's money is gone?" The money had been a considerable amount. Mitch gave Jack more credit.

"I'll say no more. I won't speak ill of the dead and he not yet buried."

Gráinne stirred out of her sleep and stretched her tiny arms. I lifted her from my lap and held her at my shoulder. She nuzzled my neck.

"She's a fine child, God bless her," Vera said.

"Two months old yesterday," I told her. Most of Mitch's family hadn't seen her. They would tomorrow, a long day for a baby and even longer for a mother who would have to make sure baby didn't disrupt, wasn't out of place.

"To baby," Vera raised her glass. She and Mitch drank.

I reached for my glass and drank quickly, unable to predict Gráinne's squirming. She might suddenly raise her head back or wriggle down my front. It took two hands to keep her secure. The sherry tasted musty. Moist dust on the glass stem stuck to my fingers. I twiddled them but couldn't rub it off. If Vera weren't there I'd scrape the cobwebby stuff onto the embossed curlicues that ran red riot over the wallpaper. The same paper covered the parlour walls upstairs, walls big enough to give the vigorous pattern and menacing colour the space they needed. In this boxroom they were on the prowl to catch and strangle you.

"But that lot were always cracked. Look at the father. Didn't he leave the land and himself idle for two years, hankering after Jack gone to America and Tom to England?"

"He missed them, Vera. He had the farm to run and both sons were gone. He'd imagined a totally different scenario," Mitch read things differently.

"If that's the case, couldn't the land be put out to conacre? No man in his right mind leaves good land to lie fallow," Vera argued vehemently as if it were happening now, not thirty years ago.

But then Vera being Vera had a point. From a small shop her own father had built a thriving business. Until Malachy did his dirty deed Vera had never known any kind of discord and was a stranger to want. Even now she lived out her days in the luxury of a fine inheritance. To her, enterprise must surely be a man's mettle.

"It was long before my time," Mitch backed away from Vera's argy-bargy.

"Sure you were only a child. The rest of us took it in turns to look after him. We had him ruined," Vera turned to me smiling at their accomplishment. I smiled back. It's what she wanted.

"We'll cut the Battenberg," Vera swivelled on the hassock and put her drink on a bundle of newspapers and magazines stacked so high up the wall they must have been months old.

She stood, twisted the handle on the door, left it ajar and disappeared down the short passage to the kitchen. The next instant two terriers shot into the room. They boogied, frisked our feet, ankles, legs high as their noses could reach then clambered onto the hassock and leapt, one to the window ledge, the other to the back of my chair. I didn't dare turn my head to look but hunched forward and sat stiff hugging Gráinne close. Behind me the dog's claws plucked the chair's brocade fabric trying to get purchase. Once still, it breathed in short pants. I pictured its mouth open, tongue hanging out drooling. At last Vera came back but she was preoccupied with the tea tray and didn't order the dogs to get down. In fact she started talking to and about them as if they were guests; uninvited, overfed and misbehaved ones.

"Don't mind your yapping. Ye'll be getting none of this. 'Tis far from Battenberg the pair of ye were reared," she gave Mitch a saucy wink and cut a thick wedge of cake giving him the end piece with extra chocolate.

I took none. The dogs' racket had startled Gráinne awake. She fussed and squirmed. I stood, patted her back, swayed and whispered sounds that normally soothed her. The dogs watched me. The spoilt pups barked jealously. Gráinne started to cry.

"Sit down!" Vera commanded. I looked at her. She meant the dogs.

They leapt at once as one onto the seat of my chair where they collided, tussled and finally settled into its webbed-out bucket hold. They rested their heads on their crossed paws, their greedy eyes on the tea tray. It was precariously balanced on the smallest of a spindle leg nest of tables. At their slightest move Vera glared the dogs down.

"You and the child have had nothing," she put it to me.

"We're fine. She'll stay asleep now until we get home," I smiled at Mitch. He got my meaning. Vera saw us to the door.

"Seeing it's a calm night, I'll walk you to your car," Vera took her jacket from the hall stand, pulled the door out after us and left the key in it. At the church gate she stopped. "I'll go in to Jack," she said.

"Then we'll see you in the morning," Mitch bent and kissed her cheek.

"Please God," Vera squeezed my arm and patted Gráinne's sleeping head.

The funeral was not particularly sad in the way a funeral is when the deceased has immediate family and lived all his life in the community. Jack had left and gone so far away so long ago he had lived, even during his lifetime, most truly in people's minds. Still the church was full as befitted the family's long standing in the locality.

An enormous wreath stood at the foot of the coffin. It was from Jack's bishop in Wyoming. Three priests who had trained with Jack and one who had flown in from America joined the local priest on the altar. Cousin Cáit sang and accompanied herself on a wheezing harmonium which she abandoned after the first verse of *Panis Angelicus*. I listened to her a cappella 'Ave Maria' from the garden outside the church where I paced with Gráinne who'd gotten restless. When the bell tolled I slipped in beside Vera and walked with all the others behind Tom, Mitch, Malachy and another cousin who shouldered Jack across the road and down a leafy laneway to the cemetery.

"Did you see it?" Vera whispered.

"See what?" I leaned close to hear her but had to be careful. The brim of her hat was bobbing. Vera was keeping an eye on everything.

"Did you see the hearse? Parked big as you please outside the church gate and he sitting at the wheel dressed black as a vulture watching to grab what he can," she did not speak kindly and brushed her gloved thumb across her fingertips demonstrating a hand itchy for money.

"There wasn't a hearse when we got here," I told her.

"I put the run on it by then so. But not without a fight," she drew the collar of her fur coat tighter and walked taller. "'Twas Malachy hired it. And for what, I ask you? 'Tis only a stone's throw from the church to the grave. 'We'll give Jack the long way round,' says Malachy to me like poor Jack's on holiday and wants the scenic route."

"'It isn't Jack wants the view at all,' I told him. 'But your friend Timmy who's looking to make a spectacle. It's a pony and trap Timmy Keefe should be driving, him with his hands out to anyone that's grieving.'

"Cute enough, didn't Timmy have the window down a crack, sitting at the wheel of that hearse listening to every word I had to say? 'I won't take that last remark,' says he and hops out onto the footpath. 'Then you can get back into your hearse and drive yourself home!' I told him. Timmy looked to Malachy for support. But just then Malachy caught sight of Father Twohy coming from the presbytery. Not man enough to do battle in the presence of a priest, Malachy backed away. And with that the bold Timmy ducked back behind the wheel and drove off in a temper, no respect for the day that's in it at all."

By now we had reached the grave site. The footfalls,

which had echoed loud on the paved laneway and crunched harshly on the gravelled path up to the cemetery gate, stopped. The air held a light mist so still I heard a bird's wings flutter before it flew out of the top branches of the horse chestnut tree that sheltered the far side of the cemetery where we gathered.

"God bless us would you look," Vera nudged me so hard I almost toppled down the tufted embankment on which I stood, one foot high, the other low, uncertain of my balance. "It's Malachy."

I looked between shoulders and over heads to find her brother and see what he was up to now. There he stood in rapid though quiet conversation with a man dressed up as smartly as he was in an expensive suit, thin tie and white shirt. They stood out from the farming men in the family whose suits fitted tight across their shoulders thickened by years of physical work.

"Who's that he's talking to?" I asked. Maybe it was he, another businessman by all appearances, who vexed Vera now.

"Talking?" Vera looked at me like I had two heads.

"Yes, over there," I nodded towards Malachy.

Vera's eyes followed mine.

"Not him," she said, "the other Malachy, Jack's father."

'But I thought he was ... "

"Dead," Vera filled in my hesitation. "And he is. Isn't that what I'm showing you? There," she raised her eyebrows and held them hard so I would look at the pile of earth heaped at the foot of the grave.

"Where? What?" I shifted Gráinne to the crook of my other arm so I could stand taller and get a clearer view. But of what?

"Those white bits turned up in the digging, they're his, Uncle Malachy's," Vera stopped as if she had clued me in.

"Uncle Malachy's what?"

"His bones," it was plain to her, why not to me? "Must be his. 'Twas for him the grave was last opened."

Prayers started and hushed her. Heads bowed. A woman pulled the two tails of her headscarf and tightened the knot under her chin. Another pocketed her rosary after signing the cross with its crucifix and kissing it. Men kept their caps in hand or on bended knee. Everyone answered the prayers Fr. Twohy intoned in a well-worn mumble. When he shook the aspersoir and sprayed holy water onto the coffin, we blessed ourselves.

People stepped aside and cleared the way for the grave diggers to come through from the back. They reached down and ran flat straps through the handles of the coffin. They grabbed hold and slowly lifted the coffin off the ground. Keeping in step as best they could given the weight they carried between them, they sidestepped up the length of the hole, two men on either side. When they bent to lower the coffin you could see the pull on their shoulders move down through their backs and into their legs. All their strength, neck to toe, was pressing hard into the wet earth, straining to keep themselves and the coffin steady. But for all their effort, the coffin bumped. The foot end of the hole was not shovelled smoothly enough. The weight of the coffin itself had to break the clods of earth that blocked its jolting way down. When Jack finally lay at rest Vera nudged me.

"Go," she said and nodded to the top end of the grave. There Malachy stooped and picked up some soil. I watched it fall and waited a second, two, three before it landed in a sprinkle of light thuds on the coffin. The distance from Malachy's hand to Jack was further than it looked.

"Mitch will do ours," I told Vera and stepped aside. Gráinne was heavy in my arms and I had already stretched the time for her bottle for too long. Besides, the ritual had brought a fulsome sense of final repose which brought death closer than I wanted. Anyway, I was a newcomer. It wasn't my place but Mitch's. Vera walked past me to file in with the others, mostly men. I went to the car to tend Gráinne. With luck she would nap when we got to Malachy's.

Cars and feet chopped the gravelled square at the front of Malachy's house. Once inside, I walked up the flight of shallow stairs smooth as the flow of an escalator and went into the first return bedroom as Malachy's wife had directed. I snuggled Gráinne under the down quilt and sat on the edge of the high bed, my legs dangling a foot off the floor. Gráinne lay on her back and kept her eyes wide open. I stroked her little legs, soothing and willing her to sleep, waiting for that moment her eyes would snap shut. Outside the window and past the outhouses in the walled orchard, apple blossoms dotted the cluster of trees. Further on, tiny daisies speckled the grassy fields where Malachy's horses stood or grazed. The daisies and the white-petalled daffodils clustered with sturdier yellow ones, sent a phosphorescent glow through the mist. It was no wonder Jack had asked to be flown back from the wide expanses of Wyoming to be buried in the intimacy of his own land.

I slid off the bed and went to the window. The maroon velvet drapes dropped below the window ledge right down to the floor. I buffed my hands on my skirt before touching the fabric and drew the drapes together. The heavy velvet shut out the lightsome damp and shut in the big bursts of golden flowers woven in giant steps all over the dark carpet.

I reopened the drapes a slit to see my way back to the bed. Gráinne's eyes were watching me. As if linked by hypnotic cord, the lids closed as she watched me come back to her side. I stood still a while and waited, then kissed her chubby cheek to make sure she was asleep before tiptoeing out the door. Going down the stairs I passed Vera coming up.

"Where's baby?" She looked at my arms, free for the first time that day. I appreciated her concern.

"Sound asleep," I assured her.

"Which bed?"

"In the first return where I was told to take her," I accounted for my actions since Vera was so keen to know them.

"The room there, behind you, with the door ajar?" she pinpointed it very specifically with her index finger.

"Yes, that's it. I left a crack in the door so I can peek in and check on her."

"We'll have to give that one a skip so," Vera turned to a woman standing two steps below her. "But what harm? It isn't the real guest room at all, not the one Malachy gives me when I stop the night at Christmas. Come 'til I'll show you." They started up the stairs past me. "But first I'll take you to the master bedroom. Malachy's after finding a four-poster, Edwardian I believe he said it is," Vera carried on. Her companion, dressed in a black twin-set and shapeless wool skirt, followed Vera avidly, both of them lusty as Malachy the morning we dropped by and found him astride his horse poised to set off on the hunt.

The large parlour was bulging with people lively with talk. I spotted Mitch over at the fireplace. Making my way to him I dodged hands holding out drinks, picked my step around legs extended or crossed from chairs and couches and sidestepped in the nick of time when a woman suddenly drew back from her companion in a burst of laughter. So intent on engineering my way unobtrusively through the jam, I didn't see her until I got to Mitch—Aunt Agnes. Mitch and Malachy were paying court to her.

Agnes was the only one of her generation still living. By default and by disposition she was the family's titular head. At our wedding I had been presented to her. Standing tall for a woman in her eighties, Agnes had looked down and surveyed me without lowering her chin. Her still wide brown eyes took in my dress. A hand was extended. Mine obeyed. I hoped it wasn't moist. There was touch but no feeling. That she bestowed on Mitch—how fine he looked, how well he had read, how proud his mother would have been had she lived to see his wedding day.

I slipped just to the right, a little behind Mitch's shoulder and stood at an awkward angle so as not to bump the flowered shade of a standard lamp already aslant. Its dim bulb shed more light than anyone would expect from me so I just stood and watched. Three red faces were talking right into each other at the drinks table, a conversation between two women on a couch kept them nose to nose and a group in a far corner kept stunning itself with laughter.

"Not to worry. We'll go into the dining-room next chance we get," Mitch half turned to me and said. He'd broken in on my staring.

"Oh, I'm just fine," I smiled my brightest to allay the awkwardness his words made me feel I was exhibiting. From her erect position on the high-backed armchair Agnes looked at me then looked away. In that moment the fire, the lamp my neck was cricked away from, the stuffy room—something—made my face hot.

Vera came in, looked searchingly around the room, landed her attention on me and held up her hand to come.

"Vera wants us," I touched Mitch's arm.

"We've been summoned," he deferred to Agnes and put his empty glass on the mantel. Agnes was not miffed.

I followed Mitch's steps to the dining-room. We joined a few others already at the oval table set for sixteen.

"They told me I'd need a winter coat and, boy howdy, they weren't kidding, were they?" A clear voice came at my side. A man's hand pulled out the chair next to mine.

"The fire's hot," I told him, glancing over my shoulder to the low flaming coals behind our seats.

"Father Kertz is my name," he twisted his large frame towards me. I recognised him from the altar.

I told him mine, almost said 'Howdy' and we shook hands.

"I ought to turn my chair around. My feet are soaked. Frozen. Numb as can be. Sure would feel good if I could just put them up there on those coals."

He would too, in a second. Priesthood had not corralled the open range of his personality.

"How'd they get wet?"

"Out in the fields. Minute I clapped eyes on those horses I couldn't help myself. Had to see them. Malachy's got some mighty fine ones. Jack always said they were dandies." He shook out his napkin and spread it over his lap.

"You've come a long way," I said.

"Wanted to. Had to. They don't come finer than Jack," the volume of his voice settled down but lost none of its spirit.

"How long did you know him?"

"He came to Our Lady's in '62. Took to him right away. One of the best assistants you could have." He picked up his soup spoon.

"How so?" I asked.

He rested his spoon hand on the table, thought a moment.

"Jack was quiet, a mild kind of guy. Nothing ruffled his feathers, not the day-to-day things anyway, or people. They came to him a lot, called him out any time, day or night, didn't matter. If there was trouble—domestic, politics, town officials, discrimination—you name it, they counted on Jack. He could spot a raw deal a mile away and he'd stick with it no matter what, as long as it took. Jack was there 'til the thing either ended or there was nothing else he could do. People didn't just count on him, they trusted him. See this?" He put down the spoon, unbuttoned the cuff of his white shirt, turned it back and pushed up the sleeve.

"It's beautiful," I stared.

He lifted his wrist and turned it slowly. My eyes were riveted by his bracelet. Made with tiny beads, the geometric pattern zigzagged in a startling interplay of rich colours.

"I haven't seen one of those in years. Missouri Indians made them too. I'd almost forgotten about them. We have them in the museum back home but they're kept behind glass. I've never seen one up close. We learned how to make them in summer camp. Ours were pretty basic, of course, always came out bumpy. Yours is absolutely gorgeous."

"It's not mine. It's Jack's. He gave it to me before he left last fall." He closed the sleeve and rebuttoned the cuff. We ate our soup.

"Is this your first trip to Ireland?" I asked.

"Sure is."

"Staying long?"

"Have to fly out again tomorrow."

We talked a little about me and home, more about him. Jack moved in and out of his conversation so naturally it was plain to see his life in Wyoming had been full and valued. In no time dessert was in front of us.

"Uh-oh. I better go. Our baby's upstairs," I pushed back my chair. I didn't like leaving. Father Kertz made me feel right at home. I wanted more than a snatch of his time.

"Where are you staying? Mitch and I have a spare bed," I offered and turned to Mitch.

"By all means, come stay," Mitch had enjoyed his company too.

"That's mighty nice of you but Malachy asked me to stay here, says there's plenty of room. He already sent his son to town to get my things. I checked into the Imperial last night."

"What time's your flight?" Mitch asked.

"About noon. Malachy says we'll get up early. He wants us to take a ride, says he has just the horse needs a heavy workout," he laughed at his own big build.

"It's too bad you can't stay longer," I said.

"Not this trip. But Malachy wants me back, says summer's the time to come."

"And by gum he's not just kiddin'," Mitch teased. They laughed. I left.

Gráinne was still asleep, her head facing straight up, her thin little lips shut tight. I put my hand on the quilt and jiggled her tummy lightly. Her eyes opened, the smile came. After her bottle I kept her in my arm and smoothed out the bed. Fixing the bedclothes was awkward one handed but I was mindful that Malachy had probably filled the house for the night and someone would be sleeping in it. I propped the pillow covered in linen and lace against the headboard. It had been alongside Gráinne on the outer edge of the bed in case she squirmed in that direction during her nap.

Up the next flight of stairs in the large bathroom I changed her damp diaper and then sat in the soft chair in the large room where a person could luxuriate and soak forever in the deep, freestanding tub. Gráinne lay on the soft, thick tufted bath mat kicking her legs and flapping her arms. She needed the exercise before being confined in the car for the hour's journey back to Cork. After she spun herself out and spent some time watching her hands we went downstairs.

Turning at the landing I heard Mitch's voice. He was at the hall door with Vera and Malachy and Malachy's wife. They were seeing off the last to leave.

"Where's the child's blanket? She'll catch her death. The draught from that door opening and closing has me frozen," Vera stood in my way, blocked me on the bottom step before I could cross the room to Mitch and the others.

"Her jumper's warm. She's in my arms. She's just been kicking. Look how red her cheeks are," I stood up for myself.

"You don't know this climate," Vera dug into my tote with such force the straps dragged my shoulder. She pulled out the lightweight blanket, unfurled it with a sharp shake and spread it across her outstretched arms.

"Give her to me," Vera commanded.

I had no choice. I handed Gráinne into the waiting blanket and watched Vera wind her tighter than I would.

"Did you see who wasn't here?" she asked as I took Gráinne back and loosened the blanket. Vera lowered her voice.

"How could I see who wasn't here?" I laughed but Vera was serious, intent on giving me the low-down on each absentee. Padge was too mean to close the shop, Christy thought standing at the church door during the removal was sufficient—"and he one of the first to write his name big and black in the mortuary book." Worst of all was a woman Vera did not dignify with a name.

"I saw herself going for messages only a quarter of an hour before the Mass was to start, just after I'd put the run on Timmy Keefe. I didn't give her the soot of looking. She was only there for everyone to see she wasn't going. As if any of us cares any more or even remembers the falling out. It wasn't even with herself. The rift was between her mother and Jack's. They were first cousins. The family never approved of the man she married—herself's father, not Jack's. There was a row one night. He was after a few jars ... here she comes," Vera stopped her story to watch the parlour door opening from inside. "The older she gets the better she looks."

I turned and saw Agnes. All at once the hall was quiet. Without actually standing to attention we all remained still. Agnes made her way towards Malachy. Her walking-stick rapped a steady pace on the mosaic tiled floor. In her elegant hand and proud posture the stick was not an aid but a stylish prop.

"You buried him well," Agnes' voice was clear and strong, used to dominating. She was speaking to Malachy.

"That's mighty nice of you," Father Kertz, standing just

next to Malachy thought she meant him. "But I only helped out. It's been my privilege to be here."

Agnes allowed her piercing brown eyes to rest momentarily on Father Kertz, the only acknowledgement she had heard him speak.

"We'll go tomorrow evening and sort out the wreaths," she continued to address Malachy as she drew nearer to him. "Those men have no sense of arrangement. Once they've put back the earth they simply toss the wreaths into a heap." She stood at the centre of her nieces and nephews who filed in respectful semi-circle around her.

"Mitch," she addressed him. "Where is your baby?"

Vera lifted the tote off my shoulder. I scooched Gráinne up the curve of my arm to make it easy for Agnes to look at her. The group watched me come close. Not sure what was expected and not having the gumption to approach Agnes directly, I took my place by Mitch.

"Show 'til I hold her," Agnes said and took two steps to us. She spoke to Mitch. As she took Gráinne from my arm, Agnes let go of her stick and without looking towards me, set it to fall in my direction. I caught it.

She drew the blanket off Gráinne and held it too in my direction. I took it. Slipping her long hands around Gráinne's torso she lifted her up just above her own face. The chandelier cast a sheen on Agnes' white hair smoothed into a knot at the crown of her head. It planted a sparkle in Gráinne's wide-open, startled eyes. All heads were upturned as if bearing witness to something ceremonial. My parents had not seen or held Gráinne and wouldn't for quite a while. Mitch's had both died. They never would. The moment touched me.

"Mitch," Agnes broke the silence. "She's all ours. There's not a bit of the Yank in her."

With that she lowered Gráinne into Mitch's arms and without turning in my direction held out her hand. I put the stick in it. She clasped its polished head, turned to face the stairs and made her way towards them. Vera dropped my tote at my feet and sped to Agnes' side.

There were quick goodbyes. Malachy's wife went to the kitchen to tend to things. Malachy took Father Kertz into the parlour for a nightcap. Mitch handed Gráinne to me and went to get our coats. No one seemed to have heard anything awry in what Agnes had said.

I opened the front door and stepped just outside. The cold air was bracing. It stung my wet eyes. Daffodils growing in pots on the two pillars either side of the bottom step stood bowed but open, their cups transparent in the strong moonlight. Daisies growing in the grass down along the gravel shut themselves in for the night. Something within each protected their delicacy from the hard frost bound to come later.

"Everything alright?" Mitch asked when he came out to us.

"I guess so," I said and started down the steps.

"Agnes is old, she ... "

"Let it rest, Mitch." There were no excuses. "This was Jack's day."

Rather than laying her in her carrycot for the drive back to Cork I kept Gráinne on my lap. It's where she belonged.

The Visitors

IT WAS NO TIME FOR A visit. We were in our new house only five days. In five weeks our second baby was due. Nonetheless Mom and Daddy came to stay with us for three weeks, their first time in Dublin.

Mitch steered the car carefully on our street. He had to turn the wheels neatly left, right, left again, to the right once more to clear the hazards. Dried up batches of mixed cement, leftover lumber pitched any old way any old place, heaps of earth, stacks of bricks and broken concrete blocks made the muddy street an obstacle course. Our house was at the end of the terrace and the only one on our side of the cul-de-sac with a roof. Foundations had been dug for the row of houses across the street. This week's rain had filled them halfway to the brim.

"This is it," I pitched my voice at a positive tone when Mitch stopped the car.

"What a pretty white door!" My Mom always finds something good.

Daddy said nothing.

Mitch went first across the lumber plank. The builders had put the plank over a gully they'd dug two days ago the morning the P&T were supposed to come lay phone cables. The cables were not down yet. Mitch carried two suitcases. Daddy followed with two lighter ones.

"We'll take these upstairs straight away, will we?" Mitch suggested in the hallway and started up. Daddy nodded and went with him. Their heavy footfalls on the bare board steps made a hollow racket. From the kitchen I could hear them overhead putting the cases down on the floor in our bedroom, the one with the half bath just off it. I had wetwashed its floor one last time yesterday trying to wipe up dust that never would be gone until the carpets came and smothered it. We'd bought and paid for them well in advance.

"You're in luck. There's plenty of that one in stock," the carpet dealer had smiled wide. "There won't be any delay in laying them," he assured us. We agreed the date—the day before we were to move in. He wrote it large on the bottom of the docket. That's the last we heard from him until last week, two days after we had moved in. He turned up on the doorstep. Mitch had phoned him from work.

"Only for this 'flu doing the rounds I'd've had a man here. I'm short two fitters," he looked me straight in the eye on the sure bet a person wouldn't call him a liar right to his face. "And the thing is I can't give you another date. I don't know when I'll have all my men back." He raised his open palms and shrugged his shoulders to demonstrate there was nothing he could do about it.

"I wouldn't mind so much but we have visitors coming. They're staying three weeks. We're living in dust," I brought the point home by rubbing my finger along the top of the hall table. Dust puffed every time we moved, had even penetrated the bedroom closets and hot water cupboard. The kitchen was tiled but I tasted dust when we ate.

"It's tough going," he shook his head. "I'll do my best for you," he shifted his cigarette into the fingers of his left hand and put out his right to shake on it. I complied but I knew no bargain had been struck. His van had not turned up since.

"Let's go see about a car," Daddy was talking again after a nap and a cup of coffee. He wanted to rent a car so as not to rely on Mitch.

On a walk with Gráinne I had seen a car rental sign hanging in the big bay window of a house on what was once a genteel square. Business must have been good. This house was one of the very few with repointed bricks, a new roof and double-glazed windows. I drove Daddy to it now, the longest ten block journey I'd ever made. He gripped the arm-rest, pressed his feet against the floorboards and braced himself tight as if we were in free fall on a roller coaster.

"Don't take your eyes off that road!" he bolted back against his seat and yelled when I looked over at him.

I snapped my head forward.

"I was just checking to see if you're alright. I couldn't hear you breathing," I talked towards the front windscreen.

"You just keep this danged thing away from those cars," he released his grip on the armrest for a moment and flung an accusing hand towards the traffic ahead and the cars parked on the side of the street.

And in that moment it all came back. I was fifteen. Daddy gave me my first driving lesson on the large parking lot at church that was also the school playground. I was awkward at the wheel but followed Daddy's directions. Even so, after starting the ignition I mistimed the clutch and killed the engine four times before the car finally jerked into action. Daddy pointed where to go so as not to distract me by speaking: straight ahead past the length of the school; turn right; across the baseball diamond; right again; steady up a slope past the convent; right; back to the starting point; stop.

Not so bad, I thought. I kept my foot firmly on the clutch to keep the motor idling. My hands were tight on the wheel and sweaty.

"You may turn off the engine," Daddy kept his face forward and spoke calmly, too calmly, like the air before a storm.

I turned the key, took my hands off the wheel, feet from the pedals and leaned back against the seat in a show of being relaxed.

"Now," he continued. I looked at him to pay close attention to the next instruction. Seeing I'd done so well, maybe he had a trickier circuit in mind.

"The best thing you can do if you want to learn to drive," he spoke slowly and kept a measured calm in his voice. I sat up a little, eager to know more, "is find someone else to teach you." He opened his door, got out and walked around to my side of the car. I realised then we were switching places. Daddy drove home.

I had been crestfallen but should have known better. When it came to driving Daddy was a fanatic.

"A car's a weapon. Doesn't matter how well you can handle it, it's the guy coming at you you have to look out for," he said any time my older brothers and sisters asked if they could use the car. When Daddy drove, even in our leafy, wide, somnolent, small town streets, he sat up to the wheel and kept himself on alert. In Dublin now, cars parked on both sides of the narrow streets, it was no wonder he tensed up.

The car dealer spotted a Yank a mile away and put on the smile to welcome him. He ran his practised eye up Daddy's considerable height and across his broad frame.

"I know what you'll want," he led us to a small connecting road off the square. For a stocky man his short steps were very quick. His fleet of six or eight cars lined the kerb, bumper smacked up to bumper. "This is the car for you," his torso went aslant when he stretched up to put his hand on the roof of a large blue Ford.

"That's the one I want," Daddy looked over the dealer and pointed to a yellow, much smaller make. Doing business he never made small talk.

Driving home my arm worked like I was slicing bread, sawing the gearstick between second and third gears so as not to lose Daddy who was tailgating me in fits and starts. He slowed and almost stopped completely for every car that came against us.

"Well done," I told him when we got home and parked the two cars side by side.

He ignored the encouragement as flattery and walked past me. Mom had been minding two-year-old Gráinne, but kept one eye out the window for us. She opened the door before Daddy reached it. He went straight to the kitchen.

"Here're the keys," he smacked them onto the counter. "You drive the thing," he sideswiped Mom and me with a look.

"The streets are narrow. Driving's tricky," I answered Mom's question before she could ask it. This wasn't the time for it.

"That and the god-danged pedals. I can't operate the damned things, they're so close together. My foot's on the brake and the gas at the same time."

So it was left to me. We had lived in Dublin only six months. I usually walked or took the bus. When I drove I stayed on carefully thought out routes and avoided the city centre entirely. Now, any place we went I drove the rented car and Daddy sat in the front passenger seat like a mountain on its volcano.

One day he bused to town and came home with an errand. From upstairs on the double-decker he had spotted a shop just before a bridge. Could I drive him to it? He didn't know its name or the name of the street. He'd taken a different bus home and couldn't recall the number because the conductor had been talking to him. He spoke so quickly it took all Daddy's concentration to figure out what he was saying. The bus number had gone clean out of his mind. But the shop was on a hill, a small shop that sold bric-à-brac. The only landmark was the canal.

I decided it was probably Clanbrassil Street and we set off. Going with the flow of Daddy's muddled mind, out of sync with the fast flow of cars, I traced and retraced Clanbrassil five times before Daddy decided we should scour some side streets. Up and down, row upon circle of red brick houses we searched.

"For what?" I finally asked. After all, I was the driver.

"A piece of copper. Just a small one," he peered out of his window.

"For what?" My mind, what was left of it, boggled.

"The clock."

Nothing ticked.

"What clock?"

"Only a six-inch strip, two inches wide. We can have it cut when we get home." The fixation had overtaken him.

I drove dumb, didn't give a hoot why he wanted copper. We would have as much luck if we stopped any old place along the canal, hunkered down on its bank and panned for gold. But I didn't dare say so. This fool's journey had backfired. Normally Daddy fired back. Here, however, in Dublin, a passenger to a daughter in the driver's seat, searching a blurred warren of foreign side streets, his mind's eye was fizzling out. I caught his real eye out of the corner of mine.

"Let's head for home," he acknowledged defeat.

"You mean the airport?" I asked, for mirth.

We chuckled. But half of us was serious, wanted Missouri.

I was the car's minder but Daddy its keeper. His father had owned the general store, was mayor of their home town in the boot heel of Missouri, and its undertaker. One of Daddy's jobs growing up was to keep the two hearses, whether idle or in use, washed, waxed and buffed bright black. He revered our family station wagon just the same, spiffing it inside and out every Saturday afternoon until you could see your face in the painted metal gleaming for God the next morning.

Mitch let the rain keep our car clean. After a heavy fall he revved the car through deep puddles that sprawled over roads that didn't drain well. On impact the puddle gushed and cleaned the car's underbelly. I naturally preferred Daddy's method but got used to Mitch's sacrilege—until now when the two might clash.

The sun came out Saturday and the men turned up to lay

the carpets so we got out of their way and spent the afternoon in the Dublin mountains, the Sally Gap and Wicklow. The hotel in Avoca did not serve dinner until eight o'clock which made us late getting home. We went to bed almost right away. Daddy didn't mention the cars needing a wash so I reckoned he was adapting.

When I woke up on Sunday and heard pouring rain I was surprised. Saturday had been such a sunny day. The rain fell so hard it sounded like a cloudburst back home where the drops fall with such force you can see them bounce off the ground. They jump higher than the steam that is released like a gasp of relief from the sunbaked streets and sidewalks. Just as suddenly as the downpour of rain, Gráinne burst into our room.

"How'd you get out?" I sat up wide awake.

"Climb," she told me with simple aplomb and walked deliberately past the bed.

"But you can't. Mitch," I nudged his shoulder. "Gráinne's out."

"Out? Outside?"

"No. Out of her cot." I watched her to prove to myself it was true. She was at the window trying to pull back the curtain.

"Did you hurt yourself?" I asked her.

"Ot-TOW!" she called Daddy's name and tugged her best at the heavy curtain fabric still trying to get them open.

"This house has gone mad," Mitch covered his eyes with his hand. "I'm suffering from culture shock in my own bed," he said, "and it's not even six o'clock yet," he checked his watch and then raised himself just high enough to plump his pillow before turning over to rest again.

Normally Gráinne woke at about seven o'clock and

occupied herself in the cot for a while. But for the past five mornings she'd been awake at five hearing Daddy go downstairs to build a pot of coffee. Mitch could turn the other way and sleep again. I couldn't so I read instead until Gráinne called and her calling got persistent.

"Ot-TOW!" Gráinne's voice was muffled. She had gone under the curtain and was tapping the window with her little fist. Just then the rain stopped. She dropped to her knees, crawled out and came to my side of the bed.

"Ot-TOW wash Daddy's car," she told me and pointed towards the curtains. Mitch's eyes shot open.

"Say nothing," I told him.

"Then you have to!" he said.

"I can't. He's my father."

I got up, took Gráinne by the hand to go downstairs but first went to the window and peeked out. The street was completely dry except for the area around our car and the rented one. There'd been no rain. The water had come from our garden hose. The sun was just coming out from behind clouds. Beads of sweat on Daddy's forehead glistened in its light. He was coiling the hose, looping it over his shoulder and around his elbow. The dust cloths I kept in the third kitchen drawer were staked with a stone on the garden wall ready for use even though a strong breeze had already dried the cars. Daddy wouldn't be happy unless he wiped over the wind's drying.

Which gave me time to dress Gráinne and have her in the high chair before he came in. She was an energetic child, always at my side insisting on helping. I used to scale down household jobs so she could help. But not any more. She could spot a makey up and didn't like them one bit.

Now she plied this big tall grandfather who had come into her life out of the blue with all her attention. I did my best to keep her out of his way. After a cabin fever Christmas two years ago, my sister had written to tell me Daddy had made an announcement to do with grandchildren. When any one of them reached sixteen, and not before, he or she could be presented to him. Until then, he preferred not to be acquainted.

Charmed at first by the crisp way Gráinne pronounced his name, he watched her every move, even sat her on his lap and held his cigar momentarily to her mouth when she reached up to take it from his. She, in turn, was fascinated with someone awake before she was in the morning, who appeared and disappeared out of the attic a dozen times a day. For right away the second day, Daddy had decided our attic needed a floor.

Walking the site he befriended two workmen. They asked his occupation and when he told them he was a dentist they asked his advice. One had a gum sore under his lower denture, the other had gingivitis. In return for whatever Daddy recommended, Blue and Red (named for their shirts) brought the best rejected timber and spare nails they could scavenge. Every day Daddy climbed the metal ladder into the attic and crawled across crossbeams to lay and hammer the patchwork of timber he hauled in from Red and Blue's rendezvous point around the back of the vacant house three gardens down. Gráinne parked herself at the foot of the ladder. She sat on the floor, her head bent back, spying up at Daddy through the hatch.

"She's pesky as the woman at Benson & Hedges," Daddy shook his jowls and all but shuddered. It annoyed him that he had to step around Gráinne any time he went up or down the ladder. The woman he referred to worked at the corner shop. The Benson & Hedges' logo hung over its door. Daddy mistook it to be the shop's name and didn't bother to correct his mistake when we told him.

The woman must have attended in the shop from its beginning. All the goods were kept on shelves that reached the ceiling behind the counter. Customers stood on a narrow passageway, the only open floor space in the shop, and waited in line for their turn to ask for what they needed. Even if there had been open access, self-service would have been impossible. Goods were shelved according to a quirky prerogative I could never decode no matter how long or hard I ran the rows with my eyes while waiting for my turn at the counter. The woman could pull products off the shelves almost without looking.

"She always gets in my way, lights on me even before I set foot in the place, doesn't even give me a chance to think," Daddy complained.

But he didn't need to think when he shopped there. Every morning he bought the same things—a carton of double cream for coffee and a selection of pastries.

"Hell! I have to fight her just to get the damned rolls I want. She tried to get me to take the ones with jelly. I told her they're no good for dunking. They gum up my coffee. That fixed her. She jumped back like she'd stepped on a snake. Can't a man dunk over here?" Maybe he should ask Red and Blue.

Daddy took shelter in church. He went every day for as long as I can remember. He wasn't pious. Nine children and his volatile emotions scared him. He looked for discipline or an anchor and needed it daily. Summer vacations we drove to

places as far afield as Wisconsin, Florida and Colorado. Every
town we stopped in, even before he found a place to stay
overnight, Daddy drove around the streets with no idea where
he was headed looking for the Catholic church to read the
sign out front and get the Mass times so he could be there the
next morning fifteen minutes late, a habit he developed after
Vatican II when a young, newly ordained priest stretched the
new rubric with such unctuous zeal he gave homilies at the
daily six a.m. Mass to a congregation of twelve.

"I go for Jesus. That fellow gets in my way," Daddy
dismissed the young one.

He found Mass in Kimmage Manor, a missionary college
near our house. Retired priests or those home for the
summer said Mass at a side altar in the transept of its small
chapel every day at ten o'clock.

"These guys know how to do it," Daddy told us when he
came back one morning. We were waiting for him. We were
going to the bank. Daddy wanted to come. "They get right
to it. Go straight to God. Keep their eyes on the book too,
don't lose their place going off on some figgery of their own,
no impromptu homiletics. Let's have coffee," he put a
brown bag on the table and did not mind when Gráinne
climbed a chair and got to it before I could. His mood was
high and we broke pastries with him, even though we'd just
finished breakfast.

"Let sleeping dogs lie," Daddy warned Mom when we got
to the bank in the village. Mom eased Gráinne off her lap
and put her lying out flat on the back seat. I parked two
doors down from the bank and waited in the car. It took
longer than I expected but maybe travellers' cheques were
tricky in a branch bank. I looked in my purse for my bank

book in case it would be needed for identification and reached back through the opening between the front seats to search the back floor. Gráinne had taken her shoes off. She would need them if we had to go into the bank. Years of practice, I knew to live in anticipation of Daddy's needs. Such a long delay or confusion with a bank teller might pull down the morning's buoyancy. I sat in readiness.

But then there they were, coming from the opposite direction.

"Know who we met?" Daddy spoke at full volume once they were back in the car. He'd forgotten the sleeping dog.

"No. Who?" I handed Mom the shoes so she could keep Gráinne occupied. Awake at once she was already interested in the brown bag on Daddy's lap and was poised to squeeze through the seats to get at it.

"Madigan. Just saw him at Mass a while ago and there he is. Turns up in the liquor store and by golly he recognised me the minute I walked in."

"Doesn't surprise me," I switched on the engine.

"No. I guess not," Daddy smiled at his bulk. "But this will."

A car let me into traffic.

"What?" I delayed asking until we were in the flow. If I could prolong whatever it was Daddy had to tell, we might make it home before traffic made him nervous or Gráinne got into gear.

"You know who Madigan is?"

"Describe him."

"Medium height. My age. A lot of hair, mainly white. Glasses."

"Doesn't sound familiar. Does he live around here?"

"Talks a lot but didn't tell me that."

"Then how would I know him?"

"If you didn't ask so many god-danged questions, that's what I'm trying to tell you."

"Okay, shoot—the answer, not me."

I heard Mom laugh. Gráinne copied her. Daddy didn't.

"Madigan's the owner."

"Of what?"

"More questions. Can't you see? It's staring you right in the face." He clutched the neck of his brown bag bracing himself against my slow mind and my quick turn around a left corner.

"Ah," I looked again at the brown bag. "He owns the off-licence."

"The what?"

"The liquor store," I amended.

"Dead right. Church every day at ten and then there he is behind the counter by eleven. And would you believe it? He tells me he owns three more."

"Right here? In this area?"

"Didn't say," Daddy dismissed the detail. "He sure is some guy," Daddy was in awe of the man.

Drink was Daddy's friend and enemy both, all through life. He had grown up near enough the Bible Belt that legal liquor or hooch, didn't matter which, and religion were ingrained as a moral dichotomy. Madigan, his feet firmly in both camps, was the kind of incongruous juxtaposition Daddy loved. They became friends. Before the three weeks were up, Madigan had Daddy on the ten o'clock reader's roster.

"Are you taking Grainy [he said it like wheat or corn] for a walk?" Daddy's tone was hopeful. He was at the kitchen table writing postcards. Mom and I looked at each other.

"Sure," we agreed automatically. We didn't mind spending an afternoon shopping or at a park though I had to watch out. After their first week with us I had an appointment with the gynaecologist.

"This is unusual so close to the end of term," he frowned when the weight bars on his stand up scales came to balance. "You've put on five pounds since your last visit." He looked to me for an answer.

"My mother's here."

His eyebrows went lower, his face showed confusion.

"We stop for tea and coffee every time we go out."

"Hmm," he was not pleased. But then how could he understand the release in letting myself be a daughter again for three weeks?

"Mail these for me, will you please? They're already stamped." Daddy handed me about a dozen postcards as he stood and left the kitchen to go upstairs for an afternoon nap. The sun was out and very warm. It had been a particularly hot morning in the attic.

"We haven't seen this much sunshine in a long time," Mom hinted. She thrives on its heat.

"Okay. We'll do a park," I was glad, easier to manage Gráinne and my weight.

I stopped at a post office on our way. Daddy had stamped the postcards, alright, but didn't know they needed airmail stickers.

"It'll only take a minute," I told Mom and got out of the car. Right or wrong I decided to find out what Daddy really thought about their visit, how much he was liking the outings, Gráinne, the house and so on. Standing in the queue at the post office counter I neatened the cards and started to read them, the first, the next and a third. I couldn't believe it. The message he'd written was exactly the same on each one. I fanned through the rest like a gangster checking a band of cash and could see at a glance that every single card said the same thing: 'Exhausted. Haven't stopped working since I got here.'

Stung, vexed, deflated, I pushed them with an angry shove into the box and went back to the car.

"You know him," Mom said. "Don't pay any attention."

Which is what he did to Gráinne during the last week of the visit. She kept persisting, lavished him with the attention he'd sparked off the day he arrived. She called to him—from her bed, from the high chair, out of the windows and from room to room. She struggled out of my hold or dashed out of my sight to go after him every chance she got.

He managed to give her the slip only once. We went to town. Mom and I separated from Daddy. We would meet for lunch. Mom pushed the stroller to keep me from any exertion that might prompt an early birth. Halfway up Grafton Street the stroller was thrust back. It jammed Mom with a force that almost toppled her. I lurched to grab her, keep her from falling. And when I did, both babies leapt— one kicked my womb and the other, having catapulted out of the stroller, was racing ahead calling up Grafton Street. "Ot-TOW!" she ran towards a large figure who ducked into a doorway and disappeared.

To the very end Gráinne didn't give up, not even at the airport when the three weeks were over. Our emotions held taut through ticketing and stalling until boarding time. There was too much to say but no way to say it. Departure loomed. Talk was perfunctory. No one's eyes dared meet anyone else's. Sure there was relief. Baby number two had cleverly stayed safe within until the coast was clear, and Mom and Daddy were going back where they belonged. Life would return to normal. But they couldn't just slip away. Goodbye had to be gone through.

Then quite suddenly it was time. We gave quick hugs that weren't nearly close enough with my enormous tummy between us. Daddy and Mom showed their tickets and went through the gateway. I couldn't bring myself to leave until they were out of sight. I stood and watched their backs move down the long corridor to boarding. My eyes blurred as I stood willing them not to turn around. I didn't want to face them leaving. But then, without warning, Gráinne cried out, "Ot-TOW! Rosie! Don't go!"

This time Daddy did not duck. He and Mom stopped. They turned as one.

I turned too, pulled Gráinne by the hand and coaxed her to come. What she and I had to face was out the other way.

The Estate

I STEPPED UP TO THE PLANK, a narrow, flexible piece of timber and started to walk across. It bounced. I teetered, caught myself by hugging the bundle of chewed up clothes tighter. The plank sank low down close to a mud puddle that spat across my shoes and cuffs. I shuffled to the end and giant stepped onto the concrete block firmly planted at the hut door. No one answered my knock. It was early morning but his dark blue Volvo was parked at the kerb. Frank had to be inside. Third time I knocked the handle thwacked down and the door opened. Frank stood there stolid, his eyes slit against the October sun and me.

"The rat was in our house last night," I got straight to the point. Greetings or soft talk didn't make sense with Frank except on Sundays when he opened the showhouse and received prospective buyers. Since we had already bought we were on bricks and mortar terms with him. Only the concrete mattered.

Frank said nothing and looked at me with dull eyes but I

knew the wheels were turning inside his head. Frank was from Kerry.

"It chewed these up," I held out the dress and two shirts. The shredded garments dangled between us. Frank put his eyes on them.

"They weren't up in the attic either. They were right out in the hall, airing in the hot press."

"Is that all it got to?" Frank nodded at the clothes. He didn't touch or examine them which made me feel crude, even voyeuristic the way I had pulled them from the press, held them up, combed my fingers through the shredded fabric stroking the full extent of the rat's greedy appetite.

"These were the only clothes in the press," I said.

"It's a good job there weren't any more," Frank finagled damage limitation and deflected from what mattered: a rat was on the loose, it had spent the night in a house with a toddler and he himself had promised, since his hut had the only phone on site, to take care of it a week ago when the rat had first found its way into attics on our row. I did not respond to his glib remark.

"Dan phoned the Eastern Health Board," he said and turned half away, reached towards his desk and shuffled loose papers—a mock show of more urgent business. "I'll look into it," he said over his shoulder, promising everything and nothing.

"But will he compensate you?" Bernie asked, her big deep voice belligerent. Bernie lived right across the street from Frank's hut. Widowed young, she had worked a full-time job and raised four children in the years before crèches, playschools and children's TV. She looked for guff and took it from no-one. Retired now, she presided over this newly built neighbourhood of eighty houses in ten terraces. Of course she saw me at the hut. Of course she called around.

"I don't care about compensation," I said and held out the plate of cookies to make amends for my spinelessness. Bernie took one, snapped it, ate it in two quick bites.

"Frank said he'll phone the health board himself this time," I told her.

"Dan-factotum on the blink?" Bernie fixed me with a wry eye and lifted the coffee mug to her lips.

Dan was a general purpose presence on site doing who knows what for who knows whom. During night watch he did nixers. For us he made and buried a block of cement to hold the clothes tree in the back garden. But the pipe he'd used to make the hole down the middle of the block was by far too wide. It gave the tree leeway. I had to hang out the wash by weight. One garment too many on any side and the tree drooped low, the clothes dragged along the ground. A strong wind set it spinning like a drunken top.

"What we need is a residents' association," Bernie said. "Frank's only playing us off each other. And there's more than this rat needs fixing," Bernie gave me a knowing look. She knew everyone's complaints. I switched topics. Bernie could quote you with a twist anywhere.

Within a week Bernie booked a room and called a meeting. A residents' association was formed. Chairman and treasurer volunteered and Bernie nominated me secretary. Of course there were no other contenders. I didn't have the gumption to say no. The meeting drew up an extensive snag list with the feverish feeling that at last we would nail Frank.

Still two weeks passed and the leaks and fissures, drafts,

faulty electrics, even the rat went unchecked. Until one day about three weeks after our meeting.

"Come," Mrs. Rosen's hand beckoned me across the street. She'd been standing at her gate and caught me on my way to the shop, pushing Gráinne in the go-cart. "For a moment only," she opened the gate and took the handle of the go-cart from me, "I will keep Gráinne here with me. You go in," she gestured with open palm and nodded towards her front door.

The key was in the lock. It was the first time I'd let myself into Mrs. Rosen's house. Normally she stood on the doorstep and gathered us into herself, guiding me by the arm, running her hand over Gráinne's hair, telling her to go to the kitchen, find the right press, open it like a good girl and take out the cake tin.

The minute I stepped inside it hit me, stung my nose, burnt my eyes, a putrid, foul odour so unlike the aromas that usually enveloped Mrs. Rosen's house, a whiff of which I could always catch from her cardigan.

"What in the world!" I dashed back to the gate.

"It is the rat. He is trapped in the cavity of the wall. Frank was here. But he only tried to make light of it. He told me my cooking lured the rat across the street, my warm wall made it welcome and it did not want to leave. 'It must have died happy,' he tried to make a joke. But I let him know he is not so funny. I told him. I said to him, 'I did not pay so much of my good money for this,'" she raised her arms in a gesture of despair, "'to live with a rat.' He says the health board will come today. But how can I wait? My stomach is churning from the horrible smell. My eyes are streaming. I must stay here at my gate."

"Come over to our house. That's how you'll wait. We'll keep an eye out for the van."

Mrs. Rosen was not upset just for herself. She was anxious about the young couple in the house next door to her.

"What if Pauline sees the rat?" Mrs. Rosen sat on the edge of her chair fidgeting with the pieces of Lego Gráinne kept giving her expecting to see Mrs. Rosen snap them together. "If she catches sight of the rat her baby will be marked."

"Marked?" I frowned.

"Oh yes. Did you not know? It is dangerous for a pregnant woman to see a rat. When she sees it she is startled, her hands fly like this," Mrs. Rosen cupped the sides of her cheeks. Lego clattered to her lap. "And her baby is born with the marks, two red spots, one here and one here," she turned each cheek towards me. "He will carry these marks. For life." Mrs. Rosen stared past me out of the window, her eyes darkening at the prospect. Then suddenly they snapped back into focus.

"The blue van," she pointed. "I must go."

For more than an hour three men from the health board, Frank, his plasterer, the electrician and Dan converged on Mrs. Rosen's house. They stood out front in her garden with their hands in their pockets or their arms folded scuffing her lawn while they watched for their turn to go inside. Each time one or two emerged from the doorway, they huddled briefly to talk.

Bernie made a beeline to the action. At Mrs. Rosen's gate where she was certain she would be seen she stopped, pulled a hanky from the pocket of her cardigan, shook it like a whip and clamped it over her nose. Billowing through the gate she drew to a halt in front of Frank. Her free hand produced its index finger and jabbed it repeatedly in Frank's face. Though muffled by the hanky, snatches of her voice carried clear across the street. Her tirade was furious and quickly spent. She turned, encircled Mrs. Rosen under her arm and swept out the gate back to camp in her house until the job was finished. Frank was not fazed by the incursion. It roused no conference with his mates who turned and watched Bernie go. She was merely a distraction from their waiting.

Coming from the shop later I saw two men uncoil a hose, drag it out from the back of the van and pull it across Mrs. Rosen's front threshold. A motor revved and pumped. Acidic fumes polluted the air. After dinner I went across to check up on things.

"In a week this will be dry and they will come to paper over it," Mrs. Rosen gently touched a patch of wet plaster on the hall wall. "I have the paper in my attic. There was some left. But," she placed a hand on my arm and held me still, "the smell, do you get it?"

I breathed deep. Mrs. Rosen had the windows and door wide open to a sharp autumn wind. "Only a trace and it's chemical, the fumigation, not the rat," I said for certain mindful that Mrs. Rosen faced a night alone—well, almost alone. Just then she ducked past me, went quickly down the hall and stood in front of the grandfather clock. Only as tall as the pendulum handle, she bent her head back to read its face. She treasured the clock, had brought it with her from the big old house she had lived in on the main road. Its ticking, she once told me, lulled her children to sleep when they were small and they had wakened to its chimes each morning.

"Two minutes to seven," she read it now out loud.

"You'd better hurry," I told her. "I can let myself out."

Without a word Mrs. Rosen went to the sitting room. I pulled the brass door handle firmly to make sure the front door latch clicked. At the gate I heard the clock chime and the signature tune ring out loud. Mrs. Rosen was ensconced in her cushioned chair to receive Coronation Street.

During the next few days Dan checked the places where rat poison had been put down. It seemed to be working. No rats were reported to the association anyway. Frank continued to ignore all other snags in our Hamelin. For three weeks he also ignored the letters I wrote and hand delivered to the hut on behalf of the committee. He didn't even respond to the one I sent by registered post.

The chairman had no choice. He called an extraordinary meeting. Right away someone demanded we put a picket outside the showhouse every Sunday. Someone else was adamant we should get a solicitor, we had a sure-fire case. One man drummed up agitation calling out time and again in a hostile voice "Go after the politicians!". But these options would give our area a bad name, a moderate voice suggested. When it came to the crunch, the meeting decided by vote that the three officers should go in deputation to meet An Bord Pleanála.

A lot of phone calls later, a date, time, even an agenda were agreed and set. But then the very evening before the meeting day the chairman and treasurer each called round and each cried off.

"Pressure of work," one said.

"A meeting came up," said the other.

"So sorry," they said.

"You'll be grand," they said.

I contacted other residents. No one was free. Bernie would come like a shot but her bellicose attitude would not enhance a wooing operation, which is how I read the meeting. Responses to my phone calls with An Bord Pleanála had been cryptic, replies to my letters telegramatic and our agenda had been rigorously combed and copper fastened before An Bord finally agreed to meet us.

At reception in the Irish Life building I was told to take the elevator to the third floor. A young woman showed me into a small conference room that overlooked Lower Abbey Street and the Customs House.

"I'll look out for the other members of your deputation," the young woman told me.

"I'm afraid I am the deputation. No one else could come." It sounded lame even before the woman raised her eyebrows.

To fortify my dispirited confidence I took the snag list from my bag and read it. Never mind the messenger, the message spoke for itself: loose ridge tiles vulnerable to high winds, holes in the pointing, brick chimneys without trays, underground pipes not lagged, boilers that would not fire, gutter clips not snapping true, no provision for ventilation in the en suite showers, a green grown derelict, kerbs crumbling ...

The door opened. Two men sidled around the long table to sit on the side opposite to me. They hugged folders to their chests the way my Dad told us to hold our cards at a poker or bridge table. Pulling out their chairs, they momentarily interrupted their mumbled conversation to nod in my direction. Three more men joined us on their side of the table. One took charge. He introduced each man by name and asked mine.

"You are here on your own," he looked over the rim of his glasses right at my face. His observation hit home.

"I'm sorry. That's just how it happened. At the last minute ... " I tried to come up with some plausible excuse when heads moved sharply and looked at me anew. At once I was conscious of two things, my foreign accent and being a woman in a man's world, busy men who carried thick folders. One started tapping the table with his Cross pen. Another looked miles past me out the large windows that glared down my back. More discomfiting was the one who checked his watch, looked at the man chairing and nodded almost imperceptibly. That nod conveyed something only they knew.

A minute passed in silence, second by second while the chairman flicked through his folder. He drew out a clean page, placed it on the table, leaned forward on both elbows and folded his fingers to rest.

"You have a few things to tell us," he invited smoothly. I saw a piranha cruising upstream. But wrong accent, feminine tone or not, I found my voice.

"I don't think we have to go through the correspondence. I sent copies like you asked. The snag list spells out the problems. I'm here for the residents. We don't believe the faults, whether they're big or small, should be our responsibility. When we go to the builder he says he will send someone around. But no-one turns up. When we persist he fobs us off, says the faults are only teething problems, they're to be expected, time will right them. People are getting frustrated. Some of them want some kind of collective action. They pushed hard for a picket on the showhouse at weekends. But then others objected, especially women living on each side of the showhouse. One of them describes us as a 'select Georgian residential area' and says she wants no talk of demonstrations outside her home. Adverse publicity isn't in our interest anyway.

"Some people said we should hire a lawyer, I mean solicitor, but even if we could agree on some action most people think it wouldn't make any difference because there are only four houses left to sell. The builder's mind is probably on his next site.

"We need to find out what the Bord's specific building requirements are in relation to our snags. And I've been asked to ask whether or not An Bord Pleanála inspects building sites. And, too, is the builder responsible for the snags? Can the Bord apply pressure and get him to take care of them?"

Glazed eyes started shifting. One man sighed. Maybe I talked too long or maybe he'd heard it all before.

"We have regulations, certainly. Our expectation is that builders will comply," the chairman enunciated in a stiff tone.

"What if a builder doesn't comply? Does he just get away with it? Can he ignore all of this?" I held up the snag list.

"One, possibly two or three items on your list might fall somewhat short of regulations," the chairman conceded that much but did not remove his steady gaze, meant to intimidate me.

"Which items? Which regulations?" I asked.

"I am not at liberty to say. They must be looked into more closely."

"'More closely' ... that means they've been looked into already?"

"The WC ventilation in those houses has come to our attention before," one man, sitting back casually on his chair, hands in his pockets, spoke to the chairman. He kept his voice low, maybe showing deference to the chairman or maybe he was revealing something a member of the public should not be privy to.

"Did a resident contact you about the ventilation? Or did one of your inspectors find it? Has it been checked into?" I asked for straight answers.

"The matter," the chairman's eyes became intensely unswerving, "is under review."

"Will that take long? The builder is almost finished and once he leaves the site, we're left. Does someone from the Bord do a final inspection?" There must be a system. I wanted to know how it worked.

"There are many builders working all over the city and we've only a certain number of inspectors," the chairman took cover.

"So. We're at the builder's mercy," I stated the bottom line as I saw it.

"Yours isn't the worst. Other builders have left houses and sites with far bigger problems," the casual man offered, as if this should console us.

"And that's what I take back to the residents?"

"You may assure your residents that we will be looking into matters," the chairman put his coping statement in place and returned the page, still blank, to its folder. His minions knew to move. The casual man, not in such a hurry as the others did not rush away.

"Good luck," he said as I walked through the door he held for me.

I'd need it.

At the next residents' meeting I made my Bord Pleanála

report. I kept it as flat as possible but even the bare facts created ructions. Legal action was ruled out. Hadn't one system already been shown to be worthless? Picket promoters demanded uncivil action but finally politicians became the target. The TD with the highest profile in our constituency had been very active lately. A general election was looming. His party was in power and intended staying there. So that a meeting with city councillors, himself and ourselves materialised, hey presto, ten days hence. This time I was not left in the lurch. Five people volunteered to come, Bernie among them.

Bernie took to city hall like a would-be councillor who feels her election to a seat in the chamber is long overdue. Not waiting to be shown to it, Bernie made straight for the main council room, picked her place and heaved a sigh that echoed round the enormous table as she sank her ample girth onto a wide chair with cushioned seat. Her head rotated full circle as her eyes toured the high windows, raked the dais and combed the four councillors, waiting like ourselves for the others to arrive, before sinking to rest in the folds of her neck. Not even the flurry of the TD's hasty arrival disturbed Bernie's roost.

All present, the meeting got right to business. A man from our side presented a well-documented case, prioritising major faults with an accompanying log of how many houses had the defects, names of residents who had informed the builder and the number of times they had done so. While pointing out the builder's nonchalance, if not total disregard, our man also instanced the dead rat in Mrs. Rosen's wall as an example of the builder's crisis management.

I was asked to report the outcome of the meeting with An

Bord Pleanála. "There wasn't an outcome," this seemed the place to talk frankly. "I asked direct questions but the answers were vague, noncommittal. I still don't have answers to what I went to find out—whether the Bord carries out inspections, whether or not they had looked at our snag list, whether anything on the list is the builder's responsibility, what recourse we have if the builder doesn't respond to us. Even when I said things are urgent, that the builder is almost finished on our site, there was no reaction, nothing at all."

"Has there been any follow up?" the TD asked.

"This," I took a letter from my folder. "A letter on An Bord Pleanála notepaper that acknowledges the meeting took place and," I skimmed to the exact words, "assures us 'matters arising from that meeting will be looked into.'"

"Is there a time frame?" The TD was on the ball.

"No."

"Is there a signature?"

"Initials. But they're scribbled. I can't make them out and there's no name typed underneath."

"They seem to be getting the runaround," The TD turned to the councillor nearest him. The councillor nodded.

"Can you track this down?" The TD pushed towards a practical course of action. The councillor nodded again.

"I can't promise anything," The TD turned to us. "But I'll do what I can to get your case priority status. Is there much of a backlog?" he asked the councillor who shrugged he didn't know.

The TD eyed him for the briefest of seconds.

"When can I expect to hear from you on this?" he cornered the councillor.

"Give us a week," the councillor offered.

"No longer," The TD tied him to it. "Is there anything else you want to raise before we bring the meeting to an end?" he asked us.

Our reports had covered everything and his directness left no uncertainties. A lot of air had been cleared. At this stage, what more could we ask?

"Yes. There is a matter I want to raise." Bernie started out of her silence abruptly like she'd held fire too long. "It's the matter of the upstairs toilet. There's no window so there's no air. After I use it I can't get the smell out. It goes through the whole house. On a warm day or when I have the central heating on, it stays a very long time," she pecked her head from one councillor to another and finally the TD, expecting an answer from each.

The chamber was absolutely silent. But like the silence after a sharp intake of breath, it couldn't last forever. When it broke I was sure some people would laugh. How Bernie might respond to that scared me. We could be on the brink of a scene.

"Councillor," the TD's voice cut the quiet. "Take down my constituent's complaint." His finesse was slick. Bernie lifted her chin. It did a lap of honour.

There was no telling whether the meeting effected any action from Bord Pleanála or Frank. Winter came and took Frank's men indoors, working to finish the final row of houses. Residents weathered the winter, brisk by day and warm inside in the evening. Interaction was minimal but twice there was a flurry of activity when central heating systems broke down and when, once again, a rat appeared. Other than that the snags went unchecked, though the TD wrote twice encouraging us to keep him informed.

The first bright weeks of February brought things out into the open again.

"Aren't so many men around the place," Bernie pointed her observation at me and poured a cup of tea at the same time. We were at her table by the window.

"You mean the builders?" I kicked to touch and took a scone from the plate she held out. I gave half to Gráinne. They were Bernie's special, baked with nubs of marzipan.

"He'll pull out before you know it. Then we're sunk."

"Not so, Bernie. The ventilation contravenes a by-law. He won't get by with that," I knew it was her chief concern.

"Hah! He had all winter. And did he put in one extractor fan?" Bernie leaned her face across the table at me.

I took back Gráinne's scone to butter it and avoid Bernie's stare. She was right but I didn't want to admit it. It would be admitting too much: that Bord Pleanala could operate as a law unto itself, ignore regulations, residents' associations, TD's; that the builder's main interest was profit; that our association had failed.

In the next fortnight the number of workmen dwindled rapidly to one—Dan, who seemed busier than ever. A note from the T.D. delivered through every letter slot told us why. The estate would be taken in charge as soon as the builder complied with certain stipulations, all to do with general outdoor maintenance. Dan got down on all fours and cleaned winter debris from the shores along the sides of the streets. He brushed up and tidied away the bits of crumbled concrete from broken kerbs and for three days running he swung a scythe at the jungle overgrowth on the green. Finally he tidied the verges, restaked the trees the wind had blown loose and mowed the grass.

His activity distracted us. Under its cover Frank deserted. The blue Volvo was never seen again. We did not know where his new site was.

But his red truck turned up a couple of days later. Out for a walk with Gráinne, she wanted to stop and watch it. Bernie joined us. The driver backed the truck close to the hut, jumped down from the cab and lowered the tailgate. Out hopped Dan. The pair of them shoved at the hut until it started swaying and then heaved it across the rim of the truck bed and jostled it into place. Dan climbed aboard. He stood steadying the fallen shed as the truck drove off.

It felt petty not to have spoken to Dan but we were mad at Frank and Dan was his man. I did wave after I saw Gráinne doing so. At the entrance to the estate Mrs. Rosen was just coming from the bus. She carried some shopping. She raised her free hand to Dan. Dan smiled and tipped the cap he wasn't wearing.

"What will we do?" Mrs. Rosen hurried to us. She was at a loss. "Dan is gone."

"Dan is it?" Bernie laughed as if Mrs. Rosen had made a joke.

Mrs. Rosen scowled at her.

"You can laugh. You are not Pauline. It is two more weeks before her baby will be born. And it is only Dan who knows where the rat might be," she walked away from us in a worry.